A Guide to

FILM and
TV COSPLAY

Calypso – Pirates of the Caribbean.

A Guide to
FILM and
TV COSPLAY

Holly Swinyard

WHITE OWL
AN IMPRINT OF PEN & SWORD BOOKS LTD.
YORKSHIRE – PHILADELPHIA

First published in Great Britain in 2021 by
PEN AND SWORD WHITE OWL
An imprint of
Pen & Sword Books Ltd
Yorkshire - Philadelphia

ISBN 978 1 52677 563 4

Typeset in 11/15 pts Sabon by
SJmagic DESIGN SERVICES, India.

Printed and bound in India by Replika Press Pvt. Ltd.

Pen & Sword Books Ltd incorporates the imprints of Pen & Sword Books Archaeology, Atlas, Aviation, Battleground, Discovery, Family History, History, Maritime, Military, Naval, Politics, Railways, Select, Transport, True Crime, Fiction, Frontline Books, Leo Cooper, Praetorian Press, Seaforth Publishing, Wharncliffe and White Owl.

For a complete list of Pen & Sword titles please contact

PEN & SWORD BOOKS LIMITED
47 Church Street, Barnsley, South Yorkshire, S70 2AS, England
E-mail: enquiries@pen-and-sword.co.uk
Website: www.pen-and-sword.co.uk

or

PEN AND SWORD BOOKS
1950 Lawrence Rd, Havertown, PA 19083, USA
E-mail: Uspen-and-sword@casematepublishers.com
Website: www.penandswordbooks.com

Contents

Acknowledgements

Thanks to Meg Amis, Margaret Swinyard, Dominic Westerland, Helen McCarthy and the cosplayers of the UK.

What is Cosplay?

Introduction

If you have picked up this book then once upon a time you wished yourself away into a world of fantastical adventure, daring heroes, dramatic space battles and dastardly villains. You let your imagination run riot so you could disappear into these stories and have the time of your life. And then you grew up. Or someone told you that you had to.

But what if that's not true. What if growing up and growing older aren't the same thing at all and actually those worlds of superheroes, pirates, space cowboys and all the rest are more within your grasp than you could have ever dreamed as a child? Well, guess what. They are.

Welcome to the wonderful world of cosplay.

A place where you can be who you've always dreamed of being. Putting on a costume can help you tap into something really special about yourself. You might just look like Wonder Woman for a weekend, but who knows, you might just be Wonder Woman every day after that. With a wide and varied community, cosplay can show you ways of interacting with the world that you may never have thought of before, and may even give you a new sense of self and inner strength.

It's time that we all woke up to the idea that playing isn't just for kids and make-believe is just as important as you get older as it was when we were five. Feeding your brain with creativity, teaching yourself new skills and opening up your space to new experiences and people are still a necessary part of our lives, and cosplay gives you all of that in abundance.

Humans love to test their brains through entertaining problem solving, interesting storytelling and most of all, through social play. Cosplay is all of this rolled into one. Learning new crafting skills like making your own clothes, working out how to recreate costumes that may never have been made before in real life (you'd be surprised how many films use CGI instead of real props and costumes these days), and getting to engage with that childish love for the imaginary again are all indispensable parts of our lives.

There is a reason that nerd culture is on the rise; no longer is it a social taboo to play Dungeons and Dragons or watch superhero movies. We all need a little bit of escapism, so it's time we all embrace our inner child and take a deep dive into cosplay and all of the amazing things it has to offer.

Miles Morales and Gwen Stacey – Into the Spider-Verse.

Pick out your favourite Disney Princess or Avenger and let's get going on how to become a cosplayer.

What is Cosplay? Looking into the Hobby

Most people involved in 'nerdom' are likely to have seen a lot of cosplay over the years, even more so in recent times as it becomes more and more popular. But even for the biggest nerds amongst us, there seems to be a lack of understanding what it actually is. And trying to explain cosplay to someone who has never read a comic book? That's even harder! But let's give it a try anyway.

So what is cosplay? That is a question that doesn't have a small answer. Well it does, in a very basic way: costume + play = cosplay. In ten words or less, cosplay is dressing up and playing at being a character, but it's so much more. There couldn't be a more succinct way of explaining it. But as with any hobby or subculture you

Cinderella – Disney.

can't boil it down to ten words or fewer. That rather misses the point don't you think? Why don't we take a jump into the world of cosplay and see what it's really all about.

If all you've seen of cosplay is pictures online, or on TV, or even in the newspapers, of people in exciting costumes, then you would be forgiven for thinking that this hobby is simply a new version of dressing up; something to get nerds out of the house every once in a while. But ask any cosplayer and they will tell you that there is more to it than going to a fancy-dress shop and picking something at random off the shelf to throw on without a thought. No, what cosplay is, is loving something so much you want to be part of it, to inhabit it, and to show that love in the most open form possible.

OK, sure, that might sound cheesy, but think of it like this: you wouldn't go and buy a football strip without already loving your team. It's important that you show your support, your passion, that this is your team, that it is part of your identity – and that's the same in cosplay. It's supporting your team and expressing your identity.

It may be that you see yourself in these characters or you connect with them on a profoundly personal level, so dressing as them is a way to open up that part of yourself. Or it may be that you want to be like them but struggle with self-confidence; you're shy, but putting on your Captain America helmet means you walk a little taller, speak a little louder, and find a way to overcome the shyness with that little bit of help from your costume. Or maybe you just really love the show, the film, or the franchise, or whatever it is so you're wearing the uniform to find your people, because that way they will see you in the crowds to make that connection. Or maybe it's because you have seen yourself as the lead on the big screen for the first time. Maybe you're the teenage girl who finally got to see Rey beat Emperor Palpatine and save the day, not only there to be the love interest, or maybe you're the black man who got to see Black Panther as king and a hero, not just the sidekick, and you want to show the world how much this means to you.

A lot of cosplayers would describe this as escapism. Which may sound as if they are running away from the world, looking for a fantasy one to live in, but the thing with escapism that you may not realise is that it isn't 'escaping' as much as being your best self. Or, in fact, finding your best self. Too often we are trapped in spaces and routines in the world that do not let us look into all aspects of ourselves; we are expected to be in a box and fit a mould, but cosplay, like all art, allows us a path to exploration of the self. With cosplay this is even more so as the aspects of escapism, such as projecting yourself onto a character, means that you are subconsciously analysing that character and your emotional relationship and attachment to them, and what aspects of them you see in yourself.

These practices are not new. In fact they are ancient and can be seen throughout human history. Pre-historical and ancient traditions all over the world involve these ideas. The folk and religious plays of the Medieval period were described as bringing stories to life through character and costume, the Venetian Carnival was a time of escapism from the rigid structures of the city laws, mummers and All Souls traditions had character performers going from house to house, and so many more practices have escapism and invocation of character at the core. The central desire that sits within cosplay and other costuming hobbies is not new, it has always been here.

Escapism in this way is more like invocation, it's more like magic. Because there is something magical about cosplay. It's not your fairy godmother waving her magic wand and turning you into a princess; no it's something deeper than that. When you make your costume you are transforming yourself. In the building of the costume you are building up aspects of yourself that either you see reflected in that character, or aspects of the character that you wish you had.

For example, you may be shy in everyday life but when you wear your Wonder Woman costume you feel as if you can do anything. You have taken the strength of the character onto yourself, made it part of who you are when you wear it. Many cosplayers find that when they take the costume off those feelings have embedded in them. The more you wear things that make you feel powerful, strong and confident, the more you let yourself inhabit that space, the more it just becomes who you are.

Helen McCarthy, author and cosplay expert, has likened cosplay to the ritualistic practises of ancient societies, where people would invoke the spirits of animals and nature to strengthen them by putting on masks, cloaks, and other items to represent those characteristics. By dressing themselves like this they took on the being of what they were invoking and were seen to become it. It made them feel more powerful in whatever situation where that extra power was needed. Cosplay at its heart is the same thing.

Doctor Strange – Marvel Cinematic Universe.

They say dress for the job you want, well cosplay is a bit like that, you are dressing for the person you want to be. No, you won't gain magic powers, but if being a superhero for a weekend helps you overcome a problem in your life, that's a type of magic.

Whether you see it as escapism or not, there will always be a certain amount of fantasy wanted in any hobby like cosplay. People want to get away from the everyday and explore fantastical lands and characters. Creating the costumes, attending events, doing photoshoots and videos lets people have time off from their lives for a moment. People sometimes just need to get away from reality. It's why we all love going to the cinema or the theatre, playing video games, or binge watching a show; it's time off from the world. Cosplay is like that but with more hot glue burns and stabbing yourself with pins.

This ethos of self-expression has led to the cosplay community housing a huge amount of minority groups; you would probably be surprised by quite how many there are. LGBTQIA+ people, disabled people (both physically and mentally), people of colour, people from different religious backgrounds; every group under the sun has found its way to cosplay. By finding their way to the community all these different groups become normalised within it. It's no surprise to see people working their walking stick or wheelchair into a costume or using a hijab as a wig with intricate folding to emulate hair.

Gender exploration at all levels is normal for cosplayers, and trying out different gender presentation with different characters is something that most cosplayers will have a go at. Because no one blinks an eye at the gender quiffy nature of cosplay lots of young trans binary and non-binary people can find themselves and explore safely within the hobby, with older queer people able to give them helpful advice without any pressure to label themselves.

There is no one type of person who cosplays and all types of people exist in the microcosm of cosplay.

Defining a word that covers so many different ideas, skills and experiences is tricky, as every single person involved will have different experiences and paths. There are many roads to take as a cosplayer. You don't have to stick to the straight and narrow (if there even is such a thing in cosplay).

There are social elements, creative elements, and educational elements which mean that cosplay can be enjoyed at many different levels. Everyone involved in the hobby finds their own way to engage with it. No one has the same way of cosplaying or the same reasons for wanting to cosplay in the first place. But at the heart of it there is the same thing: you're a nerd and you love it. So maybe one person has a need to create, wanting to make dynamic outfits and props to see how far they can push the build. They could be interested in theatre or design, using cosplay as a place to explore techniques and ideas. It may be that they have learnt dressmaking or some other crafting skills at school or with family and see cosplay as a place to explore that further. Or maybe they have wanted to learn crafting techniques their whole lives and this is the perfect chance to stretch those creative muscles.

Some will want to buy a costume and get down to the convention ready to rock, they are so eager to get into character! Buying your first costume from an online cosplay store is a great way to get into the hobby. There are loads of places that

Evil Queen (gender switch) – Disney's Snow White.

specialise in pre-made, good quality costumes straight off the shelf or, if someone wants to splash some more cash, they could commission another cosplayer to make something for them. It's like taking a first step into the pool without having to jump in the deep end with the power tools and thermoplastics. Plenty of people enjoy doing that. It's more of the 'play' element, getting your costume on and going down to the con with your friends, having a nice time and taking pictures. Plus it's not uncommon for people to buy pre-made costumes and then modify them; this is how many get the crafting bug!

Because the thing is, cosplay isn't all about the crafting and the costumes. That might sound a little weird, sure, especially considering this whole thing is called COS-play, but the hobby goes beyond far beyond both elements of the cosplay moniker. It is a social lifestyle that draws people into a community space, making friends and even finding a family for yourself amongst those who you meet in the cosplay community. Cosplay can become your life. People spend months prepping for competitions, or working on their next project for a convention; it can even become their job. With social media now so much a part of our world, many cosplayers have found global recognition for their work, and have been able to start businesses through it.

It's worth taking a look at some of the most well-known cosplayers to understand how cosplay can expand beyond a hobby. Yaya Han is probably the most famous cosplayer in the world. Even if you don't know her name, you will know her face if you have ever Googled the word cosplay. She is an American cosplayer who started way back in the '90s, and over the last twenty years has built herself into more than just a famous cosplayer; she is a brand all of her own. Yaya has been the gateway to

Doc Ock – Spider-Man.

cosplay for many people, not only through her continuous online presence over the last two decades, but also through her books, convention appearances, sewing patterns and general championing of the cosplay community.

But Yaya isn't the only example of cosplayers who have made their hobby their life. Cosplayers from all over the world have taken these steps into the limelight, and they are all great for showing how cosplay can be used as an artform, a community gathering point and self-expression. Every single one of these 'cos-famous' people have their own approach and idea of what cosplay is. Many of them, like Yaya, run businesses promoting and selling cosplay and cosplay supplies. Or they have YouTube channels and their own websites full of crafting tutorials, blog posts and more to help other cosplayers along their creative journey. They are the face of the community in many ways, so encouraging, teaching and including new people is very much part of what big name cosplayers do, playing an important role in helping beginners understand what cosplay can be.

But it's not all about fame and social media popularity. While this is a brilliant window onto the world of cosplay it is only a very small window onto one angle of the hobby. It's easy to get caught up in the bright lights of the 'cos-famous', but there are other ways to shine and express your passion through social media. Everyone has their own light to bring to the community.

Social media has made a huge difference to cosplay in general. There is a worldwide community, all interacting with each other's work on every social media platform you can think of. Instagram and TikTok have become particular hubs for cosplayers, being visually focused, allowing for a massive sharing of skills and interests throughout the community.

It can be overwhelming as a new cosplayer seeing all of this, but there's no need to panic. The joy of social media is that you can find 'your people'. Looking for a certain type or genre of cosplay tag on Instagram, finding local groups on Facebook, and getting support from these places is important, no matter what point you are at with your cosplay journey, and cosplayers are all about helping each other.

Really, the only way to understand cosplay, is to get involved. This can be online, or at the hub of all cosplay, Comic-Con.

Comic-cons are the biggest gatherings of cosplayers you could hope to find. Cosplay has become a major part of all conventions, with cosplayers coming from all over to get their geek on and parade their best and brightest creations. There is nothing better for getting to know other cosplayers and learning more about the hobby than getting down to a convention. You suddenly feel right at a home, no matter who you are. Conventions are one of the major links that holds the community together, socially, and creatively. You will meet friends you only get to see in person once a year and make new ones, and they will be friends for life. You will plan costume groups, share the techniques you learnt on your last build, gossip, laugh, do photoshoots together, holding each other's bags and making sure that your costumes looks perfect in front of the camera. You escape the world for a weekend.

In fact, due to the ever-growing popularity of the hobby, in the last few years it has become increasingly common for conventions to have cosplayers as guests.

This has opened up the hobby in a whole new way, with cosplayers doing their own panels and talks to promote cosplay to a wider range of people, interacting with the attendees, advising anyone interested in cosplaying themselves and running repair stations, help desks and the cosplay competition. That's a big deal, since the cosplay competition is one of the biggest parts of any convention, and not just for cosplayers.

In a crowded convention hall it's hard to appreciate a costume and even harder to get a good picture of it, so convention goers and other cosplayers often don't get to fully appreciate the costumes they see there. But give people an opportunity to go up on a stage, pose and act in a nice big space, showing off the costume to its best, well that's going to have people clamouring to get a seat. Cosplay competitions often get so full people have to stand!

This is the best place for taking pictures and being inspired by other cosplayers, and maybe strutting your stuff yourself.

Since they are so popular now, cosplay competitions are becoming more and more prestigious. Large scale national *and* international competitions with preliminary rounds to fight for a place in the grand final now have a place within the convention circuit; with stage lighting, set building, skit writing and performing seen as just as much part of the competition as the incredible costumes themselves. Judges will be looking for multiple skills, executed to a high standard, using pre-judging to learn all about how the cosplayer has gone about constructing every element of the costume and

their performance before they even step on stage! But this isn't how every competition works. And this isn't the only type of competition. Just like every other part of cosplay, there is something for everybody.

A cosplay competition can be anything from walking on stage in a little village hall and winning a jar of lollipops, all the way up to be being flown out to another country, like Japan, for the internationally televised final! There are even versions that are for people who don't want to compete *per se* but do want to display their costumes at their best; general masquerades or catwalk shows often happen as part of a larger competition to give cosplayers who aren't into the competitive side of the hobby a chance to strut their stuff, and also allow the competition judges time to work out their winners. It's a win/win!

No matter what convention it's at or what type of competition it is, these are beautiful celebrations of cosplay. Whether it's a competition, a masquerade or a catwalk show, people love showing off their costumes and all the hard work they put into them.

Gosh! Do you think that we have worked out what cosplay is yet? All of this, that we've talked about, is what cosplay is, but this is still the short answer. It really is a whole of many parts. Looking from the outside you see the costumes and the excitement, but pull away the curtain and you'll find all of the amazing moving parts that make up every little part of this community. It might take years and years to really work out what all of this means. And isn't that an exciting thought? Jumping feet first into a world that is teeming with passion, creativity and understanding.

Cosplay means what it means to you.

Below and opposite:
Jack Skellington –
The Nightmare
Before Christmas.

Throughout this book we are going to take those first steps into discovering what cosplay is for you, not only some of the nitty gritty of where cosplay came from, but also how to start out on your own cosplay adventure from the first moment of choosing your character, all the way through to going to comic cons, photo and video shoots and all type of cosplay related events. This book hopes to inspire you to make your own costumes no matter who you are, or how you want to cosplay.

History of Cosplay

Cosplay is a worldwide phenomenon. That cannot be denied. But where did it start out? And how did it get to be the way it is today? Did it just pop out of thin air or spring from the pages of comic books fully formed? It would be a scientific miracle if it did! Subcultures don't tend to come to life on their own, and they definitely don't become as expansive and well-known as cosplay without some good foundations and determined people along the way.

Getting Ready, Cytricon 1955.

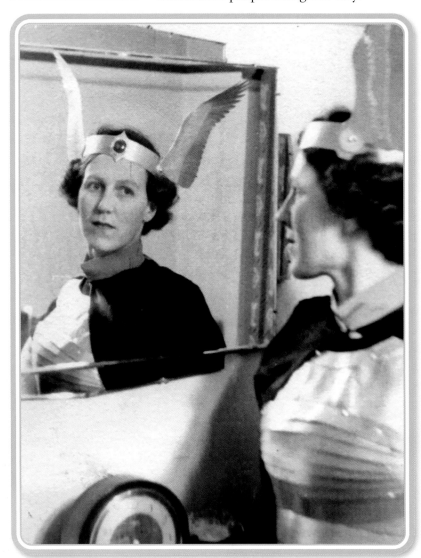

You have to know where you've come from to know where you're going, and with a community that is diverse and ever-growing, like cosplay is, keeping the history in mind means we can celebrate everything that has made it what it is.

This is especially important since a lot of cosplayers, old hands and newcomers, don't actually know how interlinked the history of cosplay is with the history of fandom and nerd culture as a whole. There is this idea that cosplay is a relatively new invention, coming along with the new wave of superhero movies or with the '90s anime fad, but this is a long way from the truth of the matter. Just because a subculture has risen into the eye of the general public doesn't mean it's new and exciting – though cosplay absolutely is exciting. In fact you can trace cosplay back to the beginning of the twentieth century, and follow the progression of the hobby right up to the present day.

While the term itself wasn't coined until the 1980s, the first costumes we would call cosplay (as opposed to fancy dress) were seen as early as 1908 and 1910.

And the very first costume worn to a convention was to the premiere World Science Fiction Convention (World Con) in 1939!

So no, cosplay did not just burst out of the ground at some point in the 1980s, fully formed and ready to go. Just like any subculture it was born from many moments of societal change, people reacting to what was happening, and a love for what they were doing.

But we've got ahead of ourselves. Let's start at the beginning.

Ballet at Coroncon 1954.

Costume Pre-1900

The thing to realise when thinking about cosplay is that, as long as there has been popular culture there has been cosplay, and as long as there has been media there has been some form of popular culture. From ancient folk storytelling to the musical halls of the Victorian era, from the groundlings of Shakespearean London to the Kabuki theatre of Japan, there has always been a version of popular culture as enjoyed by the populace, which means there has always been some form of fancy dress.

There is something about costume and performance, and not just on stage, that entices human beings. It's magic made real, invoking spiritual ideas that connect us with the world around us in the form of physical storytelling. Live the story and you understand it better, and you understand your place in it better.

Ancient people would use animal skins and masks to draw the power of animals and spirits into themselves, believing the costume of the creature would imbue them with its characteristics, and isn't that what is wanted when you wear a cosplay? To feel like that character and take on their traits as well as just their appearance. You do it enough times and you actually start to have that belief that this is who you are. An old idea with a new face.

One of the most famous historical uses of costume that mirrors the cosplay conventions of today is the Venetian Carnival. Carnival was about becoming other people; the masks and costumes gave people freedom and the space was almost a world apart from everything of the regular. During Carnival the sumptuary laws (laws to try and regulate consumption) were suspended, allowing people to dress how they liked no matter their social class or job within the city, as these things were usually tightly regulated. The wearing of masks and costumes to become a new person for the period of Carnival gave people freedom beyond what they were used to and the Carnival became infamous.

The Carnival had, and still has, classic characters that the famous masks represent and are not just random costumes. Many of these costumes that were worn at Carnival were characters from the *Commedia Dell'Arte*, such as Colombina and Pantalone, each having their own characteristics that people would take on when they wore the classic mask and costume. Just like cosplay, right?

This is still part of the spirit of the Carnival to this day, and it's not uncommon for people involved in modern day costuming hobbies, including cosplay, to travel to Venice to join in the celebrations in the traditional fashion.

And it wasn't just the Venetians who liked a fancy-dress party. Masked balls and masquerades have been popular amongst the wealthy and aristocracy for centuries, and with everyone else too, if and when they could afford it. Louis XIV was infamous for his balls and his costume of choice, the Sun King. This costume was based on that of Apollo, the Greek god of the sun and the arts, and in this costume Louis would perform for his guests.

Queen Victoria held many a costume ball during her reign. One of these balls, which was recorded by the painter Sir Edwin Landseer, was an attempt by Victoria and her husband Prince Albert to help revitalise the Spitalfields silk industry, instructing all the guests to have their medieval inspired costumes made from the silks. (You might have seen the episode of ITV's *Victoria* about this.)

These occasions were for fun, frivolity and, to a greater or lesser extent, the enjoyment of anonymity. Being able to play at being someone else for an evening, much like at the Venetian Carnival or our modern day costuming events.

Towards the end of the Victorian era, fancy dress parties were becoming more and more popular with the middle classes, and large masquerade balls were held for people to attend. And it was at one of these masquerades, in Washington State, that the first glimmer of the cosplay we know and love today was born.

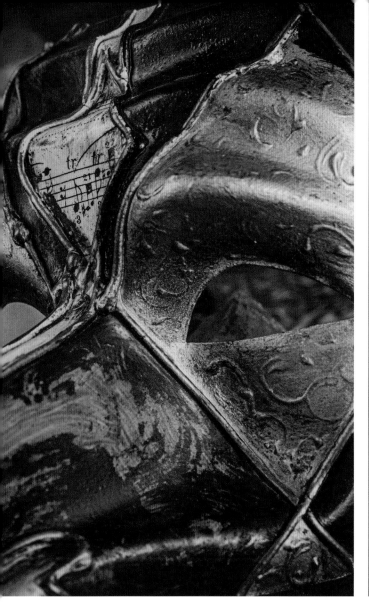

1900–1950s

At the turn of the twentieth century, the world was turned on its head. There was revolution in every aspect of society. A new time, with new ideas, new gadgets, gismos, and a whole new outlook on what the world should be and what could be achieved.

It was a period of great change, and with that change came one of the biggest differences in how people interacted with popular culture: the beginnings of a mass media. (Obviously nothing important happened before we had TV.)

Almost overnight (well over a few decades but, in the grand scheme of human existence, that's pretty quick) there was a massive influx of new media and new ways to interact with that media, the most influential of which was the wireless. Inexpensive to produce and accessible to almost everyone, wireless radios meant instant entertainment. Radio allowed for the creation of things never attempted in theatrical productions, such as science fiction. You didn't need theatre sets or costumes, you just needed a mic, a sound booth, and a bunch of creative sound effects. The opportunities were endless.

Group of Costumes at Cytricon 1956.

At the same time, books, newspapers, comics and magazines were exploding in popularity; people wanted more content than ever before. Serialised stories had been popular in newspapers for years, for example Charles Dickens' novels were printed as serials for mass consumption, but as literacy rates rose the demand for exciting, enthralling stories of all forms became higher and higher. Comics, in a form that we would all recognise, popped up in every paper, and started to get their own dedicated publications.

It is actually from one of these serialised comics that what could easily be called the very first cosplay comes: *Mr Skygack, from Mars*. The title character from a popular comic strip featured in the *Chicago Day Book*, *Mr Skygack* ran from 1907–1911, and may well claim the honour of first popular culture alien, as well as being the first cosplayed character. The costume itself was made and worn in 1908 to a masked ball in Monroe, Washington, by William Fell. He even won best costume.

Couple this explosive desire for mass media with the upswing in available education for all and people having spare time for leisure activities, and you have everything needed to create modern popular culture. These new characters being dreamed up in the media provided new inspiration. They captivated people. Finding out what happened next was as important then as it is now; they probably had 'no spoilers' rules too if they missed an episode and had to wait until the Sunday rerun.

Not only were people excited to listen to or read these stories, they wanted to be part of them. There was a demand and desire for fans to show their love for the new media in brand new ways.

Enter sci-fi and literary conventions. Or what we would call Comic Con. Conventions such as World Con provided a new space for shared discussion, artistic expression and open admiration of these stories, and of course, there was cosplay.

Myrtle R. Douglas, known by her nickname Morojo (Mō-Rō-Jō), turned up at the first World Con in costume, along with her partner and fellow fanatic, Forrest J. Ackerman. Until recently Ackerman has been credited with being the first cosplayer, but it was Morojo's designs and crafting work that they both sported, and which really deserves that credit.

The pair shook the newly developing sci-fi scene with their outlandish future fashion, based on the movie of H. G. Wells' *Things to Come*, dividing the other con goers on whether this was an amazing new part of the celebration of pop culture or not. Some saw it as silly and childish, but many jumped at the chance to express their passion for pop culture through what quickly became known as fan-costuming.

By the second World Con, dozens more people had started making their own fan-costumes and Morojo even ran and hosted the first ever costume contest for the hobby in her hotel room at the next World Con. This competition would later become a staple and fan favourite of World Con proper, on the main convention stage. The competition runs to this day.

Morojo continued wearing her own designs and costumes to World Con, as well as pieces made by the likes of Ray Harryhausen, in her ongoing effort to promote fan-costuming. Both on and off the convention scene her passion for the hobby could be seen in the many sci-fi 'zines that she wrote and edited for over the next 20 years.

While fan-costuming took hold in America in the '30s and '40s, it wasn't until 1953 that it appeared over the pond, at the London Science Fiction Convention. Unfortunately, this was not fan-costuming in the strictest sense as it was part of a performance.

The Second World War had rather gotten in the way of people running and attending literary and sci-fi events in Europe (honestly, how dare it!) so hobbies such as fan-costuming, which was and still can be expensive and time consuming, didn't get a fighting chance until the '50s and '60s.

Wins First Prize As "Skygack"

Times readers don't need to ask who the dickens this is. Sure, It's Skygack from Mars, one of the Times' humorous characters. August Olson of Monroe, Wash., contributed the picture. He "made up" as Skygack and "copped" the first prize at a masked ball at Monroe.

Mr Skygack Costume 1908.

Morojo and Forrest J Ackerman at the first World Con 1939.

Lois Miles posing at World Con in 1949, continuing the tradition.

L. Sprague
de Camp
←

L: Bob Briggs
Center: Willy
Ley
←

At the
Masquerade

Fan-costumers at
World Con 1952.

Scene from ballet
"Asteroid"

Inventive costumes and a panel at World Con 1954, much like modern conventions.

In 1955 the Liverpool Science Fantasy Society attended the first Cytricon wearing home-made costumes and, much like Morojo, carried the trend forward and encouraged others to do the same.

The next few years saw the first ever cosplay masquerade in the UK, when World Con was hosted in London, followed by EasterCon in 1960 which had a costume party and a competition as part of its official programming. It's safe to say that fan-costuming had made its mark on the UK convention scene and was here to stay.

Having fun in costume at Coroncon 54 and Cytricon 56.

In the 1960s the small fan gatherings of the early conventions suddenly become a thing of the past. No longer were they few and far between with only a few hundred people (if that) gathering together; no, with the '60s came a whole new type of comic con and whole new wave of fans ready to strut their stuff in costume. Conventions started popping up all over the place in the UK and Europe. People had money to spend now the shadow of war was gone, and pop culture was going through a transformation, with television zapping new life into science fiction. The sci-fi of early comic books and radio shows had no choice but to make way for a fresh vanguard of serialised TV shows such as *Star Trek* and *Doctor Who*.

Andorian alien – *Star Trek*.

Star Trek fans were very quick to jump onto the costume bandwagon, having fan-costuming as a major part of their events. *Star Trek* conventions were some of the

first to not only have a basic masquerade but to have a proper competition, a fashion show of fan designed and created collections in a similar style to fashion week, and have large amounts of floor costumes, where you wear your costume on the convention floor all day rather than the costumes being there just for the masquerade.

This may have been because of the influence of earlier convention goers, especially from America, sharing their experiences through fanzines (this was the equivalent of a forum or fan site before the Internet) as well as their own anecdotes, thus inspiring the introduction of costumes and masquerades earlier than other fandoms in the UK and Europe.

Trekkies have always been amongst the most passionate of fan creators. It would not be an exaggeration that without the dedication that was put into the fanzines and costuming events of early *Star Trek* fandom we would not have the nerd landscape we have today. (You cannot ignore that the first real fanfiction was written by trekkies after all!)

The *Doctor Who* fandom, while slower to catch on, has made up for that with utter staying power. You can't go to a convention today without seeing a *Doctor Who* cosplayer, be they classic or Nu-Who. Daleks and Doctors have been gracing convention floors for the last 50 years in one way or another: even in the wilderness years of the '90s when *Doctor Who* was off our screens, fans were wrapping themselves up in tinfoil and heading off to show their love for this giant of pop culture.

Comic books also gained a new lease of life.

The 'Silver Age' of comics, as it is now known, was in full flow by the mid 1960s, drawing in bigger audiences with a new interest in the medium. Many of the earlier comics had fallen out of favour, as with larger than life, almost god-like heroes making up much of the content they felt out of touch and unrelatable. The Silver Age revamped older characters or saw the creation of new ones who would become household names in the years to come, such as Spider-Man and the Fantastic Four.

Comics in the '60s and '70s found a new way to connect with their audience, not through shows of strength but through emotional pathos and empathy. This was the era that made the comic book heroes we still enjoy today.

For costumers this meant not only exciting new costumes but also seeing the influence of new subculture fashion movements in the '60s, '70s and into the '80s, like punk, goth and the new romantics, being reflected in the designs of characters. Costumers really got to start stretching their creative muscles, working out new ways to recreate these costumes with a whole new wave of fashion wear, fabric types, wigs and more.

These changes in media led to an upsurge in interest, not just from existing fans, but from the new upwardly mobile and more socially aware teenagers of the 1960s and '70s. A youth interest in comics that spoke to them drew this new group of pop culture enthusiasts to conventions and costuming events, helping them to grow in size and popularity beyond anything the early days of World Con and fan-costumers could imagine.

Lucca Comic Con, now the second biggest convention in the world, started in Lucca, Italy in 1966. It drew people from all over Italy and soon from further afield to a town-wide celebration of pop culture. The convention takes over the whole of

Fan-costuming at Large, Bullcon 1963.

The Invisible Girl – Marvel Comics.

Victoria – *Heart of Empire*.

Lucca's historic centre and is not just one of the largest but one of the longest running conventions in the world.

In the 50 years it has been running the convention has successfully made cosplay one of the most prominent parts of its five-day celebrations, with large scale sets from films, video games and cartoons for taking photoshoots, a costume parade throughout the town, as well as a costume competition that is infamous for how in-depth and detailed the costumes, judging and performances are.

But none of this is anything compared to the monolith of pop culture that was about to appear. The 1970s heralded the arrival of an event that would change what conventions were and a name that would be known to nerds for decades to come: San Diego Comic Con.

San Diego, and its predecessor New York Comic Con, crossed the streams of pop culture. They took the comic book events and the sci-fi events and did both together, networking with large fan organisations outside of the comics sphere to help grow the events. This brought in a whole new crowd to the convention scene and started to join up the gaps in existing nerd culture. They also encouraged big name production companies and studios to advertise their films, such as *Star Wars*, at SDCC and NYCC.

We can't talk about the history of cosplay and not talk about *Star Wars*. It would be like talking about the Renaissance and not mentioning DaVinci. *Star Wars* was a cultural phenomenon; people flocked to see it, and the two sequels. And so did cosplayers, jumping on to the costumes in these films so fast you could even call it light speed.

Above and opposite: Star Wars is one of the most popular franchises of all-time, inspiring legions of fans.

The likes of X-Wing pilots, Imperial Stormtroopers, Luke Skywalker, Princess Leia and Han Solo quickly became costume staples of conventions. Everyone wanted to be part of *Star Wars*, and much as with the comics of the '60s and '70s, these characters prevail to this day, with their successors from the prequel and sequel trilogies being just as popular amongst cosplayers. *Star Wars* even has its own dedicated convention, Star Wars Celebration, for fans and cosplayers to show their love.

There is a lot of cosplay folk lore surrounding *Star Wars*. People going to see the films multiple times taking all the notes they could about the costumes and props and pausing grainy VHS tapes of the movies to catch glimpses of costumes from every angle.

The costume makers of this era were amazing in their ingenuity, creativity and determination. The whole process was harder. Beyond having to sketch references with a torch in the cinema, none of the amazing range of fabrics, materials, wigs, make-up or SFX that cosplayers are used to today were available; many didn't even exist. People had to use their best *Blue Peter* brains to get stuff done. They innovated in ways that modern cosplayers would just take for granted.

But it wasn't all *Star Wars*, new wave superheroes and conventions cementing their place as bastions of nerd culture. One of the most important moments in the history of cosplay happened in this era, the coining of the word cosplay itself.

In 1984 Nobuyuki Takahashi, writer, producer and founder of Studio Hard, attended the 42nd World Con in Los Angeles as a university student. He and his friends were already aware of costuming at events, as it had started to become common at Japanese conventions in the 1970s, but World Con had always been a world (hah!) of its own when it came to costuming. Inspired by what he had seen, Takahashi, upon his return to Japan, wrote a piece in the *My Animé* 'zine, creating the word cosplay to go with it.

Fan-costuming, hero-play and masquerade were the terms most in use at this point but when Takahashi translated this into Japanese he found that the word felt 'too noble

Below and opposite: Costume makers strutting their stuff in the costume masquerade at World Con 1965.

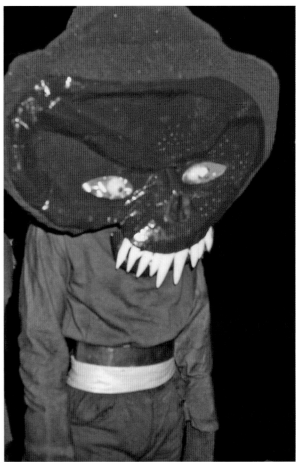

and old fashioned' (quoted from Brian Ashcraft's book *Cosplay World*, featuring an interview with Takahashi) so felt that a new, youthful way to describe it was needed to really describe the hobby. Taking the terms that he'd come across at World Con Takahashi finally settled on the word cosplay, a perfect mix of the art of costume and playfulness of the activity.

Cosplay became a sensation in Japan and by the time the next Comiket, the biggest Japanese convention (and now the biggest in the world), rolled around, people from all over Japan attended in costume. This was the beginning of the global cosplay community, a cultural crossover that sits at the heart of modern-day cosplay.

Despite all of this, cosplay was still not the popular hobby it is today. It was not until the arrival of another technological advancement that cosplay would really blossom: the Internet.

Up until now there was no way for cosplayers to connect with each other. They met at conventions, wrote in 'zines and communicated in smaller groups but for the most part these would be contained within their own country, often just their own town or city. But once the Internet crashed onto the scene everything changed. Forums dedicated to fandom sprang up, and within them cosplayers started to chat, share and eventually make their own forums and websites to gather more like-minded people. Cosplayers were finally able to understand that they were part of a global community.

With the Internet, the seeds of fan-costuming that had been set way back in the 1930s by Morojo and Ackerman, and the deep roots of costumes in the convention scene, were about to bear fruit.

2000 to Present

With the beginning of a new century a new wave of cosplay would break. It's suddenly cool to be a nerd. Superhero movies and comic books are back in fashion in a big way, the sci-fi classics of the '70s and '80s are nostalgic and people want to play Dungeons and Dragons again. TV shows like *Community* and *The Big Bang Theory* have brought the loveable, passionate nerd up to date and everyone is obsessed with *Game of Thrones*. The twenty-first century is the century of nerd culture, and cosplayers are there to ride the curve.

Joffrey – *Game of Thrones.*

Technological advancements online meant that the global cosplay community was able to start huge amounts of cultural exchange and break down the walls of this illusive and exclusive hobby. They could finally go beyond posting 'zines to each other and actually build a hobby that happened two weekends a year into something more. But this online world of cosplay allowed for more than just those who were already aware of the existence of cosplay to find each other: it also meant that people who might never have known about conventions, let alone cosplay, could interact with it for the first time. And not only could they interact with it but newcomers could also learn how to get involved. The Internet gave cosplayers a chance to share their wealth of creative crafting techniques online.

YouTube and blogging sites made it easy to post and find information about every aspect of cosplay. Whether you are looking for a tutorial on a new technique, want to read about experiences within the cosplay sphere or want to see reports, images or videos from conventions and events, everything you could want to find about cosplay is now just a click away. There are forums and groups on social media sites to help cosplayers with their build progress, supporting each other and creating global communities within their members. Many of these groups will be able to help find high quality reference images for costumes, or simply use Google to hunt down images in a quality cosplayers of the past could never dream of. You can find pictures that are so high resolution you can even zoom in to see the weave texture of the fabric! The wonders of modern technology.

But the Internet didn't just allow a space for connecting with other cosplayers. With the rise of social media, cosplayers were able to start sharing their work with the nerd population in general and create fan bases all of their own. A lot of cosplayers like to share their hard work to larger audiences than just their friends and family, and the likes of Facebook and Instagram have allowed them a global reach. It has led to some cosplayers becoming almost as, if not more, famous than the characters they are cosplaying, engaging with thousands of fans around the world.

But it's not the just the Internet that has changed cosplay. The advancements in materials available have meant that cosplayers can now reach new heights with thermoplastics, LED lights and miniature smoke machines, 3-D printed parts and props, and new fabrics that were either too expensive or simply didn't exist until the last 20 years. And do not underestimate the difference that the availability of global delivery has made. Being able to get wigs, materials and fully made costumes from all over the world for reasonable prices has made cosplay more accessible than ever before. Technology has drawn the community together to become more connected and more collaborative, sharing information, materials and a passion for the hobby.

Conventions have gone from strength to strength. San Diego and its ilk have become Meccas of pop culture, with hundreds of thousands of people flocking to them every year, but outside of the large scale conventions you will find a myriad of smaller events such that, in the main 'season', you would now be able to go to a different convention every weekend.

Despite cosplay having a history and presence just as long as conventions, it wasn't until the late 2000s that cosplayers were really taken seriously as part of the convention scene. For a long time the costumes were begrudgingly included with a masquerade, but a lot of con goers saw cosplay as a frivolous part of nerd culture. Something entertaining on the con floor but otherwise a bit silly. In the last two decades, cosplayers have fought back against this, solidifying themselves as an important and credible part of the convention scene, with the competitions becoming massive draws, and cosplayers themselves being offered slots as panellists and guests as part of promoting the hobby.

Did you know that there is a cosplay competition that is essentially the Olympics for cosplayers? The World Cosplay Summit (WCS), started in 2003, takes place in Nagoya, Japan every year, with cosplayers from all over the globe competing to be known as the best in the world. The cosplayers who make it to Nagoya must have first won in their own countries for the right to represent said country at the finals. With cosplayers performing multiple times in brand new costumes, constructed purely for this competition, the World Cosplay Summit brings the most inventive costume and performance elements of cosplay into the limelight. It even has a flag ceremony.

The WCS may be the biggest but it is not the only competition of this type. There are several other high level competitions both international and national. The European

Above and opposite: Ghost Rider – Marvel Comics.

Above and opposite: Luke (on a Tauntaun), Leia and a Wampa – *Star Wars*.

Cosplay Gathering and the International Cosplay League are both incredibly prestigious as is the Chinese International Cartoon and Animé Festival (CICAF) Competition. These competitions do not just give cosplayers the chance to compete around the world, but also have huge cash prizes and rather excellent trophies – which is definitely a perk.

Cosplay has got to the point that there are now conventions purely for cosplayers, with location and set shoots, informative panels and workshops to level up skills, dealers' halls with cosplay related merchandise and much more. Cosplay has become a fandom in and of itself, away from the main body of pop culture.

One of the more interesting side effects of cosplay's current popularity is that cosplayers are being considered in the designing of new characters for all sorts of media. Lots of companies have started to realise that having people cosplay their characters is good for them so some have started using cosplayers in their design teams as consultants. It's not uncommon for a games company or a marketing team on a film to contact cosplayers to help in the promotional work of a new product. Cosplayers can often be seen gracing the red carpet of film premières like *Star Wars* or *The Avengers* to bring a little extra pizazz to the occasion. A company may commission a large scale build of a new video game character to walk the convention halls, drawing in new customers. It's a great time to be a cosplayer.

Black Panther – Marvel Cinematic Universe.

Cosplay seems to be getting bigger every day. It's been reported on national and international media, there are TV shows about it, major theatre, film and TV studios are hiring cosplayers to work in their costume departments, and institutions like The British Museum are starting to see cosplay as something to take seriously and be involved with. Cosplay has grown far beyond the small subculture it started as. And there's no stopping it now.

Cosplayers are finding themselves at the forefront of pushing what costume and pop culture can be, but they always have been. The hobby may have grown but the core passion is the same and that is what will drive cosplayers to continue innovating and invigorating pop culture. What does the future hold for cosplay? Who knows, but it will definitely be creative.

Different Types of Costuming – An Intersectional Subculture

If you've ever Googled cosplay, it's almost a certainty that you will have come across multiple costuming hobbies in your search as well as cosplay-based information. Cosplay is only one part of a large alternative costume scene that crosses into other areas such as alternative fashion and burlesque. These all heavily borrow from each other and all have similar roots in theatre, music hall and artistic expression using your appearance.

Hobbies such as LARP (Live Action Role Play) and historical re-enactment have been interwoven with cosplay for decades; you are very likely to find that people from all of these groups have at least tried their hand at one of the others or may even still do them alongside each other.

You might even have seen alt-fashions/lifestyles like steampunk, Lolita, drag and more intersecting with cosplay. The design elements of these alternative fashions crop up all over the cosplay community with people doing versions of characters inspired by their favourite alternative fashions or subcultures. Making what's called crossover costumes like steampunk Iron Man or zombie stormtroopers are very popular, with artists, developers and costume designers in the media making official versions of these types of designs for cosplayers.

LARP, historical re-enactment, steampunk, and alternation fashions all have a place in pop culture and while all of these hobbies and lifestyles are very different they all cross paths, and have similarities that bring together a love of creativity, eccentricity and self-discovery.

Here's a quick overview of the wider costuming communities and subcultures that you can see, and what to look for if you are interested in finding out more or how they differ from cosplay.

Drag

Drag is one of the oldest forms of costume and performance. There is not a period in history where some form of drag was not part of the entertainment of the time, though that might be being slightly hyperbolic. The style of drag that we recognise today comes mostly from the Victorian music halls and the likes of Vesta Tilly (one of the most famous early female drag performers), William Dorsey Swann (a gay rights activist and former slave known to be the first person to describe themselves as a 'queen of drag') and the pantomime dames of the late Victorian and early nineteenth century pantomimes who were part of creating the over the top image of the drag queen that we know today.

Drag at its core has very similar aspects to cosplay, especially cosplay skits and competitions. It is a performance art that conjures up the ideals and flaws of our society through escapism, as well as nurturing a place of acceptance for people who feel outside of their community for whatever reason. The exploration of gender,

Drag is all about self-expression and creativity.

presentation, and messing with the *status quo* sits at the heart of drag performance, and while many only see the surface level of rude banter and lewd comedy, drag challenges people to look deeper into themselves and find a new, better version of who they are, much like cosplay.

Drag queens and kings have always borrowed from popular culture to create their acts, riffing on the celebrities or commonly known characters of the period, and while they create exaggerated versions of them, they have embodied the characters as much as, if not more than, cosplayers.

In the last few years, with *RuPaul's Drag Race* and other drag centric media becoming more popular in the mainstream, cosplayers have not only started including more drag elements, like the OTT make-up, wigs and padding in their costumes, but also started to celebrate the queens and kings themselves by cosplaying as their personas! It truly is an exchange of art and ideas.

Historical re-enactment

Historical re-enactment or living history has been around at least as long as cosplay has. Some of the first recorded re-enactments happened in the 1600s and it became incredibly popular in the nineteenth century as the Victorians became obsessed with romanticised versions of medieval history, crusades and the art of chivalry. In the twentieth and twenty-first centuries re-enactors have moved away from the fantastical and romanticised versions of history, putting their effort into accurate recreations of the past to educate people in an immersive fashion.

Much like cosplay, re-enactment does not have any strict rules to what you have to do to get involved and no particular period or place that you have to adhere to. There are always going to be some periods that are more popular than others, in the same way that Spider-Man and Harley Quinn are pretty high up on the list of who people want to cosplay, but you can find groups for almost any historical era no matter what takes your fancy. Classical history through to modern age World War re-enactment, there's something for everyone.

People all over the world are involved, often travelling to places to join in on large scale events, such as the Jane Austen festival in Bath. Flocks of Regency re-enactors can be seen walking the streets for the whole of the festival, with public and private talks, dances, picnics and more happening for days. In America many cities hold Renaissance fairs, and while these are not re-enactment in the strictest sense, and are more in the Victorian romanticisation area of things, they are incredibly popular. Big, family friendly events encourage people to engage with the hobby and hopefully the history, though sometimes it's more about the knights doing a bit of jousting.

Re-enactment does focus more on the accuracy and educational elements, but there is still a lot of crossover with the cosplay scene, not least that a lot of the first cosplayers were re-enactors as well! There is still that same urge for escapism, to experience a different world away from your daily life, and the same passion for the subject matter as there is in cosplay. It's community, comradery and creativity, just this time with a Napoleonic uniform on instead of a Star Fleet uniform.

Above and opposite: Historical re-enactment of the early Tudor period.

LARP

It's a big game. Really. LARP falls into the big melting pot of roleplaying games, along with tabletop games like Dungeons and Dragons and online RPGs like World of Warcraft. All of these games fall under the banner of roleplaying but LARP takes it to a whole new level. Bringing in elements of re-enactment and cosplay, LARP integrates the love of costume and performance with the more story driven elements of roleplaying games. Much as with Dungeons and Dragons or any of its contemporaries, LARPs have a game master who, along with a team of helpers, will set up the world, create the story elements that are required for the main game (though players will be able to create their own stories within that), organise the events themselves and everything that goes with that and generally make sure that everyone is having a good time. It's a pretty full-on hobby whether you are a game master or a player.

Often LARPs have fantastical or magical elements and settings, but like their tabletop counterparts, this is definitely not always the case. You will be able to find or set up LARPs about every genre under the sun. This being said there is usually a structure for the LARP which people work within. Grand Fairy Balls, noir detectives solving puzzles in old warehouses, zombie survival runs, Lovecraftian horror, games played through sending letters to each other, these are all LARPs in their own way. People have started creating online LARPs through apps like TikTok, so anyone, anywhere can join in with the game! In fact you could even call escape rooms small scale LARPs since they include many of the same elements, and people have started dressing up to really get into the spirit of things. So don't for a second think that LARP is just hitting each with foam swords and yelling 'fireball!'

LARPers will spend hours, upon hours creating characters, backstories, relationships and alliances within the game, and community and character is of huge importance to them. While you are in the game you must stay in character and only break character in designated areas, and if you're killed or similar, depending on the game set up, you have to start from scratch! New character, new start.

Considering that you will have made a costume, spent time and effort getting attracted to this character, there is a big emotional connection in LARP that you may not have in cosplay in the same way. This is literally putting yourself and your passion for the game on the line. But it's always fun being able to make someone new too!

A lot of cosplayers take part in LARP events since there has traditionally been more free range in character design and the way costumes are made in LARP circles, though the two are starting to blend together more and more now that people have started to realise you can cosplay characters of your own design. For people who aren't so interested in the game side of LARP, cosplaying as your own Dungeons and Dragons character or similar is a happy medium.

Steampunk

Part costume, part historical, part art, part fashion, all eccentric. Steampunk is retrofuturism at its' best. Imagine if the technological revolution of the twentieth century happened in the nineteenth and the whole thing was steam powered. Getting to the moon – steam powered; computers – steam powered; cybernetics (even though we

still aren't quite there) – steam powered! This is an art movement inspired the by the fashions of the Victorian era, combined with sci-fi of H. G. Wells and Jules Verne, and the aesthetic of early cinematic and illustrative visualizations of the future.

It's easy to get involved in steampunk, and as with cosplay and other costuming hobbies there are plenty of online groups and forums to dip your toe into for advice and inspiration for your first look. Getting hold of second-hand bits and bobs to make up an outfit is a really great start, because you don't have to be making mechanical dragons or hydraulic armour straight out of the box. There are loads of great shops that cater for steampunk fashion, so you can look fancy straight away, but the real joy of the steampunk scene is the freedom of design and creation it fosters.

Artists, like Herr Dokter and Dr Geoff (who actually earned his PhD as he likes to remind people), create artworks in all types of media. From working sculptures to cartoonish, cheeky prints and patches, steampunk encourages people to explore beyond the everyday. You can find steampunk being created on YouTube, in comic books, in fiction and even in music. Steam Power Giraffe, an electro-vaudeville band from San Diego, describe themselves as 'a musical act that combines robot pantomime, puppetry, ballet, comedy, projections and music', all under the steampunk banner. And we couldn't mention steampunk without talking about the one, the only, Professor Elemental.

It could be said that Professor Elemental, with his multiple viral videos, brought steampunk to the attention of the wider nerd culture, and definitely was part of cementing it as a major part of pop culture. His rap style music videos, playing the role of the grand British eccentric with a punk rock twist are a great way of getting an idea of what steampunk is in a three to five minute portion.

While steampunk is obviously its own genre within costuming, cosplayers borrow from it frequently to bring new life or an exciting twist to an existing character, rather than doing original designs like steampunks do. The clockwork and steam-powered elements really lend themselves to designs like Iron Man or stormtroopers when cosplayers are looking for an original twist, whilst also being respectful to an equally creative hobby. Give and take within costuming hobbies is what makes them so much fun, bringing together ideas to make new and better ones, experimenting with how far things can be pushed and developing more ways to create these amazing, wearable works of art.

Alternative Fashion

Alternative fashion falls adjacent to the costuming hobbies rather than necessarily being one of them. You tell someone who is part of one of the alt-fashion subcultures you like their costume and you might not be giving the compliment you think. However a lot of these fashions inspire cosplayers in their original designs/re-designs of characters, much like with steampunk and, of course, there is the same desire for self-exploration and expression.

There are practically as many different subcultures as there are people involved in alternative fashion, but some of the big ones are the Japanese Lolita style (no, not like the book), cyber punk, regular punk, goth of all shades as long as it's black, fairy-kei and vintage. If you haven't heard of one or any of these let's have a quick run down!

Lolita

This is a fashion originating in Japan and has strong ties with the Harajuku district of Tokyo. It is based on French Rococo design and the childhood fashions of the Victorian era, with an emphasis on 'cuteness'. The fashion can be divided in three main styles: gothic, classic and sweet, though there are many other sub-divisions such as sailor, punk, military and country.

Though the fashion has the same name as the book *Lolita* by Vladimir Nabokov, the book has no bearing on the fashion as it grew out of the 'kawaii' movement in the '90s, with young women taking control of their autonomy through their femininity in all aspects of their lives, including clothing. Lolita has been likened to the punk movement in Britain for its self-expression and escape from the *status quo*. In fact one of the most prominent designers for the punk movement, Vivienne Westwood, designed a staple of the Lolita wardrobe, the rocking horse ballerina shoe.

Punk

Punk is a revolutionary arts movement that started in the 1970s and '80s made up of music, fashion, and DIY art. It is known for its plaids, ripped up clothing, safety pins and dramatic, dyed hair styles. While it has moved on in the last 50 years, the core areas of the fashion are still visual in modern punk, with people still embracing the DIY attitudes into their lifestyle and not just their clothes. Punk was a reaction against the establishment, built on ideas of anti-authority, non-conformity, anti-capitalism, do-it-yourself attitudes and direct political action to bring about change. Though it is the fashion that you will able to clock at first glance, the dance, literature, visual art and specific type of music that was created within the movement are just as vibrant and expressive as the clothes.

Goth

Goth is punk's 'edgier' sister. A subculture that celebrates all things dark and spooky, goth brings in elements of the punk scene's attitude and mixes it into a pot of literature, horror stories and classical art. Goth is almost synonymous with the scarier side of alt-fashion. Dressed in black, with the stereotypical pale make-up and dark eyes, the truth is that goths are probably more likely to mother you and give you a cookie than cast a hex. Like Lolita, goth leans on the fashions of the Victorians and Edwardian eras but has taken its favourite parts from every era it has survived through and added them to the creative melting pot.

But, as with every alt-fashion there is plenty of variation for people who don't want to look like Lydia Deetz from *Beetlejuice*. Pastel goth has become a huge side arm of this fashion, flipping the script and playing the traditional gothic styles in bright pastel pinks and blues, and 'prep' style goth, inspired by '90s film fashion has definitely found a place in the gothic fashion canon. If you see any goth look, you'll get an experience of all sorts of luxurious fabrics. It wouldn't be unusual to see velvet, lace, silk and fishnet all work together fabulously in a gothic outfit. Films like *The Coven, The Addams Family* or *The Crow* are mainstream must sees for anyone wanting to get an idea of this sub-culture before taking a deep dive into the dark world of goth.

Cyberpunk and Cybergoth

A sub-division of the punk and goth fashion as a whole, the cyber versions have rather taken on a life of their own with clear visual styles and trends. They incorporate elements of goth, punk, rave, and industrial fashion. Both cyberpunk and cybergoth are inspired by and give inspiration to a huge amount of sci-fi literature, comics and games, even lending their name to the game *Cyberpunk 2077*. You can find the stylistic traits in the films like *Blade Runner, The Fifth Element, Mad Max, Minority Report* and more.

Fairy-Kei

Another style from the streets of Harajuku, fairy-kei is a playful, colourful and exaggerated fashion that draws in elements of childhood fun and cartoonish imagination. The style is heavily inspired by cartoons of the '80s and '90s, *Polly Pocket, Rainbow Brite* and *My Little Pony* all hold a place in the hearts of fairy-kei enthusiasts. Like punk bright, over the top hairstyles are a huge part of fairy-kei, with layers of cute hair clips covered in cakes, sweet treats and cartoon characters decorating the hair to push it into exciting shapes and exaggerate the hair and face. Most fairy-kei has a colour scheme of pastel colours adding to the childlike wonder of the style, as well as including chunky jewellery, oversized t-shirts and long socks, paired to large light-up trainers or similar. If you ever wanted to look like strawberry shortcake, fairy-kei is the way to go.

Vintage

Vintage style, not vintage values. It might feel that when you see someone dressed in clothes of times gone past that they wish they lived in another era, but celebrating vintage style is far from backwards looking. There has been a massive revival in buying vintage and second-hand clothes in order to help the planet and that has led to the vintage fashion scene being more popular than it ever has been. People are rocking their best rockabilly selves, heading for tea in tea dresses and reliving the Jazz Age in their best top hats and tails.

There is an urge to lump vintage fashion in with steampunk or historical but the fancy dressers of this alt-fashion are more interested in restoring the looks of the past with a modern day attitude than re-enacting it. This is fashion rather than costume, and for many it's their everyday wear and not just for special occasions. With festivals, parties and events all over you are never far from pulling out a boater or dusting off the tweed, ready to hit the cocktails.

Vintage 'Chap' fashion.

2
SECTION

Character and Design

Getting into Character

Starting your first costume can be a daunting task. It's all new and big and exciting, and maybe a little bit scary, but do not worry. We have all been there. All those amazing cosplayers you see online or at conventions, they were all once where you are now, wondering how to take that first big step. They all took a deep breath and that first big step into cosplay, picking the character they most wanted to be. And golly it's a big thing to think about, but the wonderful thing with cosplay is that there's always another event, another convention, another costume. You don't have to pick just one.

You can definitely do more than one costume at a convention no matter how experienced you are, most of them run for two to three days after all. And some even have after parties and evening events to strut your stuff in another incredible creation. Plenty of time to make and build, and many, many conventions to go, so actually it's a pretty good thing if you're never out of ideas of what to wear.

There's no need to get worked up about your first costume being the perfect choice or the perfect build. Cosplay is, at the end of the day, an art form, creative and exploratory, so it's all about you doing what you want, your way, and making mistakes of any type is a big part of that.

On the other hand, it would not be a surprise if at least one of you reading this had a bit of a panic and your mind went blank the moment you tried to think of someone. Don't panic! We can go through the process of working out a character together no matter which end of the character picking spectrum you lie at. Hopefully you'll feel completely confident in your choice and be ready and raring to go by the time the crafting starts!

Everything in this section is advice. Like any art form we all find our own process – these are just some ideas to get started.

Valkyrie – Marvel Cinematic Universe.

Reasons for Picking your First Character to Cosplay

The obvious thing to say when picking your first cosplay is 'pick your favourite character'. Easy, obvious, to the point. Cosplaying as your favourite or one of your favourite movie or TV characters is a sort of a no-brainer and probably part of the reason that you want to start cosplaying in the first place. You might have that character jump straight to the front of your mind when reading this and know right away that you want to be them. That's awesome! But sometimes you might need to go deeper than that. Some people have lots of favourites and it's like picking between your children which one you want to make first. Or that character that appeared in your mind's eye has a costume that you aren't quite sure how to make or where you could buy it. It can all get a bit much. But never fear! There are lots of ways to get yourself going on that first costume adventure. So if you are feeling overwhelmed, just follow through these ways of choosing a character and you'll be over that first hurdle in no time. And if you aren't, these are some great ways of thinking of more cosplays for the future.

Daenerys Targaryen –
Game of Thrones.

Before we get started...

If you have some ideas already, jot them down. Now. Go on. Don't overthink it. Good. That list is a perfect starting point to work out who you want to be. OK, we'll be coming back to that. Let's go!

Do you like/relate to that character's personality?

While a character may not be your 'favourite' for other reasons, sometimes there will be ones who you relate to on a personal level that mean a lot to you. Your favourite

Darth Vader – *Star Wars*.

Star Wars character might be Luke because you saw the original trilogy as a kid, but Rey means more to you as an adult/teen because you relate to her more. This doesn't stop you loving Luke but cosplaying as him may not be as special to you as cosplaying as Rey. It's simply a different exploration of what you want to get out of your cosplay experience. This doesn't stop you cosplaying *both* Luke and Rey either; there is always more time to make more costumes.

It may also be that you like a character because they are interesting to you. This is particularly the case with villains. If we stick with the *Star Wars* references, Darth Vader isn't exactly a good person but he has a lot of interesting things going on with his character, backstory and motivations. You don't have to want to blow up planets or be a space dictator to like his character and want to cosplay him. A lot of people cosplay as characters who may have some moral lapses in judgement, or are straight up evil, because they can really get into the part, think they are well written or just think they are interesting characters beyond being the hero. And it's great fun to be the bad guy.

Do you like/relate to them for physical reasons?

While you definitely shouldn't think you have to physically look like everyone you cosplay and nor should you feel you have to cosplay someone purely because they have similarities to you in appearance, it can be

Queen's Guard – DC Comics' *Wonder Woman.*

really exciting to see someone who looks like you on the big, or small, screen and want to cosplay as them. This doesn't mean that you are a 'look-a-like' for that character, though that does happen, it may be that they have the same body or hair type, skin tone, gender and so on.

Lots of girls and women cosplayed Wonder Woman and Captain Marvel after their films came out because they loved seeing women as superheroes when most superhero films have male leads. The same with Black Panther and *Enter the Spider-Verse* for black cosplayers. These moments of representation mean so much that people got to see themselves as characters that cosplaying as them was a must.

Of course, there are ways of making yourself look more like the character you are cosplaying. Make-up transformations are really popular with lots of how-to guides online, but looking like a carbon copy of an actor is most definitely not a must for when you pick a character. But let's not use make-up to change your skin tone, eh? That's not a good look.

Do you like the costume?

This may seem obvious but liking a character's costume is a big part of cosplay. You may have a character who you love but you don't like their outfit for some reason. Liking a character and liking their look are not mutually exclusive things; it may be that your favourite character in a film has a costume you don't like or don't fancy making but you like another character's look. That's fine, and you are completely valid in your choices. Sometimes you see a costume and the aesthetic, artistic side of your brain goes 'WOW I WANT TO WEAR THAT!' without you even knowing who the character is or what they are from. There's nothing wrong with that either. You liked how it looked and that's awesome!

Do your research and enjoy making the costume; you may even find that you like what the character comes from and find some new media to fan over.

On the other side of the coin, if there is a certain reason why you don't like a character's outfit, for example maybe you don't want to wear a skirt that's on the short side, or it simply has elements you don't personally like, you can change that up. Adding your own changes to a costume, and giving it a redesign is a really big part of cosplay, so if you like a character, but don't like their look why not try doing some sketches of how you could make it work for you or have a look around to see if other

Elphaba – *Wicked*.

people have done designs that you like more. There are so many out there and it's a great way to give yourself a creative challenge.

Do you like the show/game/comic/other media?

Sometimes you just love a show and you want to be everyone and everything in it. And sometimes that show/film/game/whatever doesn't have standard types of characters. *Tetris* or *Pac-Man* are perfect examples of that. But you can still cosplay from it. Go right ahead and make all the characters or maybe even cosplay something wacky like a human version of a computer or a weapon, or recreate a non-human character as a puppet or something exciting like that.

Or maybe that show doesn't have 'characters' in the traditional sense, it's more like a reality or talk show; that's not a problem either. There's been a bit of an upsurge in

The Sanderson Sisters – *Hocus Pocus.*

people cosplaying as contestants from *RuPaul's Drag Race* for example and it wouldn't be unheard of to see someone dressed as The Stig from *Top Gear.* Where there's a will, there's a cosplay.

Sometimes groups of friends want to do a big character set together; this can mean that you might have to all compromise on who gets what character if you have collectively decided that you want to try and do a 'full set'. If you and a friend both like the same character, you can decide between you who gets to do that one and then help the other pick a different character that they also like from the show/film/game/whatever. Because you are all fans of the same thing, it's really fun to do it together and this won't restrict you maybe switching in the future or doing your favourite character another time. Make sure you all talk about it before and agree everyone is happy doing the group this way first, as you don't want anyone getting upset because they couldn't be the character they wanted.

It's also worth remembering that you don't have to be restricted to one character, or even to any characters. If you love the film/show/game/whatever you work out how you want to cosplay from that even if it's really off the wall!

What crafting skills do you have?

Remember that list we made? How's it looking? Has any of this helped you pinpoint what you want to make? Or has it just made the list longer? Well, that's no bad thing.

It's definitely not uncommon for cosplayers to have a long list of characters that they want to cosplay, so you'll be in good company as you work through it. But it might help if we look at things from a slightly more practical side for a moment.

For a lot of people making their first cosplay is the first time that they have used a sewing machine since textiles classes at school, and you may never have used foam or a heat gun, so it's worth taking that into consideration. Take a look at your skills, what you can already do and what you want to learn, then check those things against your list too. If you have no idea what you're doing when it comes to crafting, don't worry we'll get to that and if you have some clues of what to do and where to start, you can use that as part of your first build.

It's worth remembering that, while you should consider what you are currently able to do, this should not restrict your ideas or your vision for your cosplay. Pushing the boundaries of what you can make and learning new skills is part of what cosplay is all about. There's nothing wrong with deciding to take it slow and steady, levelling up your crafting ability with each costume you do, learning from your mistakes and rectifying them for the next build or the next section you're making. It might mean starting with a smaller, less flashy character so you have a costume ready for Comic Con, but you'll definitely have a skills bank to be proud of in a few builds time and a steady base to continue improving from.

Or you can go big or go home! Make that Iron Man suit, sew the Padme Amidala lightbulb dress! It might seem like a leap into the unknown but you can learn just as much by putting all your effort and drive behind a big build straight away. Be prepared though, you will need time and focus to get through a large-scale crafting project, so maybe don't try and do it for a

Below and overleaf: The Queen of Hearts – Alice in Wonderland.

deadline. You'll be learning every step of the way, and it may take longer than you think but it will be absolutely worth doing.

Or you could do both. Have a large build in the background while you practice with, or buy, smaller ones and still have a costume to have fun in at cons.

And lastly…

All of the above

All of these reasons, or any other reason for picking your character is valid. It's your costume and you should enjoy making/wearing it no matter what.

If you have a list that is longer than your body, or just one fixed idea, those are both awesome and that's the beginning of your cosplay journey. Going through these ideas should really help solidify what you want out of your costume and how you want to go about doing it. It's never going to be the same for everyone. Some people will want to make as many different characters as they can and always have something new, others will want to improve on just one costume for each new convention, and there will be people who fit all the way along the spectrum in between. What's important is finding your space, your way of doing things and enjoying that process. Picking and putting a costume together is meant to be fun, so if you aren't having fun doing it one way, try another.

And speaking of that, it's about time we started looking at how to put your costume together.

Wormtail – *Harry Potter.*

Reference, Review, Repeat

Yay! Cosplay picked! Congrats for getting past stage one. Now the hard work begins.

When you are planning your costume you need to decide if you are going to aim for a complete, accurate replica of the costume as it is seen on screen, or if you are going to use that as a starting point and add your own flair. For either option you are going to need reference images.

It might seem obvious but collecting your references is an important part of any cosplay build.

Even if you have made more costumes than you can count on your fingers and toes, each time you start a new costume you are going to need to know what it looks like; it's simply going to make your life easier. Having a good amount of reference images, designs, sketches and more makes a massive difference to your ability to craft something you are proud of and which looks exactly how you imagined it. Working from memory will only make things more difficult, and the likelihood is that you will have missed some elements of the costume because you haven't been able to see it from all angles or close up.

If you are making a costume redesign or original design for a character, having references of their original look will add to your knowledge and help you retain the spirit and overall recognisability of the character in question. You don't want to end up redesigning them so that no one knows who they are anymore.

Either way, prepping with references will make all the difference to your build.

Finding Images

We live in a modern age of wonderful things, like the Internet and full HD stills from every film and TV show under the sun. Long gone are the days of pausing your VHS to squint desperately at an angle of a costume you hadn't seen before or taking notes in the cinema on your fifth viewing of a film to work out a fabric type. No, now all these reference images are at your fingertips, if you know how to find them.

Whether you are going to make your costume from scratch, collect pieces and modify them or buy a pre-made costume, having these references will mean that you get the best chance of having your costume exactly how you want it. And if you are commissioning someone to make it for you, the more references you have the happier the commission maker will be with you because they will know what they are doing and don't have to do that work themselves. You want the perfect costume? You've got to do the leg work to get it. Who said this was going to be easy!

A good Google search for high resolution screen shots is always a good start. It's very likely that once a film or TV show is out on a streaming platform or BluRay and DVD there will be hundreds, probably thousands, of screen shots from it that you can find online without much effort. This of course does mean searching through these thousands of images to see if what you are looking for is there. This is still a very time consuming method of finding references but if you are aiming for 100% accuracy with a costume it's definitely one of the best ways to find all the information you need. Looking through screen shots will mean that you get to see the costume in different lighting, you will get different views on it including close ups and full body shots, and you'll be able to see what it looks like when the actor is moving.

The joy of this is that you can see how costumes have been made to achieve certain things, such as combat scenes or dramatic/dynamic movement, like a cloak swirling around. You may only notice extra panels or layers of petticoats in these moments of captured movement.

Often having a moving clip or gif of how the costume moves can be just as helpful as a still image. This will give you even more of an idea for working out the fabric type you might need as you will be able to see the movement repetitively.

Sometimes film and TV show production companies will release the original design artwork or full body turn arounds for people to use for cosplay. This is becoming more and more common as a lot of companies and content producers have started to realise how useful and profitable having cosplayers dressed as their characters can be. For a myriad of reasons companies want to encourage people to dress as their characters, and that is no bad thing to take advantage of as a cosplayer.

If you look on the website for a film or franchise you may be able to find these released images, or there may be art books of the production you can get. If you're lucky, your fandom might have a costume designer or part of the costume team who is happy to talk with fans and share images. *Game of Thrones* costume embroiderer, Michele Carragher, is well known for sharing her work from the show and chatting with fans who want to have a go at recreating her costumes. If you are going to email or message a designer, don't make assumptions. Ask them first through a medium like Twitter if they are open to talking, if you haven't already found any clear answer on their social media pages or websites, or if they are open to requests for costume images. And always be polite in your request.

And, this may sound silly, but you can also use things like action figures of the character to find out details you may not have noticed before. Having a good action figure that you can turn around in your hands and physically hold can help see a seam or the back of a hat or a pattern on armour that you may not have noticed before. Disney merchandise is very good for this, especially the *Disney Princess* dolls and *Star Wars Black Series* range of figures.

You can never have enough different types of reference.

Doing all the prep work with references not only means that you have them all available if you want to find out what one thing looks like but it also helps you get a clear image in your head so that you feel confident in your build. If you're doing your own design work you'll need this even more as it will help you gain that feel and understanding of the character beyond the stylistic and key points of their costumes that are a big neon sign of who the character is, such as Captain America's red, white and blue stars and stripes.

Knowing how their costume reflects their personality, their 'job' (this can be anything from a witch to an astronaut and back again), and how they fit into the world

Above and opposite: Sansa Stark – *Game of Thrones.*

around them, will inform your own creative process. Taking all of these things into consideration is important when you are doing your own versions.

If you are doing a more screen-accurate costume, the references will mean you will have a full understanding of the garments or armour pieces that make up the costume by helping you understand how it was made, what layers go where, and the tricks that have been used to get the costume to sit how the designer wanted. Also it means you can get in really close and have a look at the fabric to see what the grain is like, or how a piece of embroidery has been done, even seeing how the chainmail has been made.

Is it Secret? Is it Safe?

OK, you don't need to keep your reference images secret. In fact it is actively encouraged for people to share their finds to help out other cosplayers who may be looking to make the same character, but keeping all your references somewhere all together and safe is a good idea. Plus who doesn't like a *Lord of the Rings* quote?

Creating folders, both physical or digital, of your images makes a build so much easier from the get go, and having them close at hand throughout is important for not making silly little mistakes with how something looks. We've all rushed through a piece of sewing or painted a design without checking and been annoyed at ourselves afterwards for not having the reference to hand.

Some cosplayers will have printouts of the costume references stuck up on the wall or a corkboard as they work so they can constantly check against them that they are doing the right thing. Others will have a physically folder with plastic wallets to flick

Star Wars helmets.

through all the images they need kept in their workspace, or a digital version on a tablet or laptop. Some find that having a sketch book where they draw up all the ins and outs of the design, including things like harnesses to hold parts in place or under garments like corsets so it all fits properly, to work out how the costume works helps them get everything just right. Or people do a mix of all of these. Everyone has their process.

The brilliant thing with having these reference folders, however you like to have them, is that when you go shopping for materials, patterns and general haberdashery add-ons and the like, you can take all those pictures with you. You can check all the fabrics you look at against your images until you get exactly what you want. Making sure you have the right buttons is easy when you have the reference in your hand, and you'll never get the wrong paint colour if you can swatch it against your print out. You can even keep all the samples you get in it if you can't make up your mind in the shop or have to search for materials online.

The usefulness of the reference folder cannot be understated.

If you are planning on entering competitions that require workbooks, these physical folders and sketch books are also a really good way to start getting into the habit of recording your work in progress too.

Keep it all safe and sound.

Always Ask for Help

When you are making a costume your biggest asset is other cosplayers, so don't be afraid to ask for help.

The point of the cosplay community is to be there for each other. Cosplay groups and forums are there to help you in your build progress. With a quick search on Google or Facebook you are likely to find a group dedicated to cosplay from the fandom you have chosen, so you can see how others have made/put their costumes together. Or you can find a group/forum dedicated to cosplay builds of all sorts to get more wide-ranging advice like how to use a certain material or sew a certain type of fabric. Places like the Replica Props Forum can be good for this, or the UK Cosplay Community and the She-Props community (though as the name suggests She-Props is a safe space for women and non-binary cosplayers). These are places you can ask for advice, find other cosplayers who have made similar or the same type of builds, talk, learn, find tutorials and so much more.

Much like when asking a costume designer for advice, if you ask a cosplayer about their build by messaging them or talking privately, be polite. Ask if they are OK to help you out first on an image of their costume or in a private conversation, instead of bombarding them with questions out of the blue, and it will really help both you and them if you make sure you ask a specific question rather than, 'How did you make X costume?' as that is a very large and open ended question. Many cosplayers do it as a hobby and won't be able to tell you everything they did in a costume build; either because they do not have time, or they didn't record the process in any major way. Try asking about a certain part of the costume you are struggling with or the fabric or materials they used for part of it that you haven't been able to work, or the patterns for creating the garments or armour. These are all much more specific and tailored questions, which means that the other cosplayer will be more likely to have the time to answer your question and there is a higher chance of getting the help you need. They may even be able to give all the information you need from their own reference research. But also, don't be upset or offended if they can't help you. You can always try and ask someone else or look in a different group for advice. Not everyone is going to feel confident enough in their process or have the time at that precise moment.

Accuracy vs Modification: The Big Fight

A lot of the reason for collecting reference images is to make your cosplay as accurate to the original costume as possible. It can be a challenge to aim for this level of recreation, but is it always the best way to go about a cosplay? There is some debate in the cosplay community about whether striving for accuracy is something that should be held above other forms of costume making, or if it can be harmful to the community's inclusive nature.

One of the main parts of being a cosplayer is your self-expression. It is the core of the hobby, but in the last few years, as cosplay has become more popular, especially as something for other people to view rather than get involved in, there has been a push towards people being perfect doubles of the characters they are portraying. Cosplayers who are look-a-likes for actors, or are very skilled with make-up transformations (an impressive talent, there is no denying) have been held above other cosplayers often by those who are not cosplayers themselves but are viewers and fans of the hobby. This has, in some ways, pushed for people to look and be a certain way in the hobby, rather than just enjoying themselves and creating the costumes they want to create.

Unfortunately it is not just people outside of the hobby that have fallen foul of the lure of complete accuracy. Some cosplayers, in their desire to be as 'accurate' to a character as possible have used offensive stereotypes of racial costumes as well as makeup and prosthetics to change their appearance to that of another race.

This is called race-face, stemming from black-face: the act of a white person using make-up to portray a person of colour. This has sparked large scale debates on what is appropriate in cosplay across the whole global community, with the majority calling out race-face as unacceptable.

It may seem obvious not to use another person's race as a costume but the need for complete accuracy has enveloped parts of the community so much that even skin colour becomes part of it.

This is not to say that accuracy in a build is a bad thing, not at all. There is a huge amount of skill and ingenuity in recreating a costume, that has likely taken a whole team of professionals to make, in your shed. Cosplayers find the most inventive ways to piece costumes together from a handful of images and a collection of parts from the local DIY store! Some have gone even further by making costumes that were never even real, like the Iron Man suits which for most of the Avengers films are CGI, but leave

The Predator – *Predator*.

a cosplayer alone for long enough and they'll be walking out of there in a wearable, working suit. It's creativity at its finest.

On the other side of this, the cosplay community, as ever, has rallied to a call of inventive inclusivity and in the last few years there has been a surge of support for modifying, re-designing and creating original design costumes. People are celebrating cosplayers of all genders, skin colour and body type, and the way that they portray their favourite characters no matter what.

Finding a way to put your own stamp on a character sets a challenge all of its own. Just the same as with any artistic skill, learning to design your own stuff, even if it's just

Vanellope – *Wreck It Ralph.*

making small changes, can take time. This doesn't mean learning to draw, because you don't have to be good at drawing to be good at designing, only you need to understand what you mean; it's more about learning how to draw the threads of ideas together into a coherent design. When you are designing a costume, having knowledge of things like fashion trends, historical and futuristic designs as well as art and design styles beyond just clothing will mean you can really let those creative juices flow.

Even if you fancy doing a fully accurate build there are always options to change things up with the design to suit you and your needs more, whatever they may be:

- You may want to make the costume more flattering for yourself; say the skirt is very short on the original design and you aren't comfortable with that, you can make it longer and it still be an accurate recreation of the costume but you are happier wearing it. Your comfort and enjoyment in wearing your cosplay is more important than that costume being exactly how it's shown on screen.

Storm (Gender Switched) – Marvel's X-men.

- Your favourite character might be a different gender, so a re-design could be as simple as changing their gender without changing anything at all about the costume other than fitting it to your gender instead of that of the original one, or you could do more exaggerated changes like maybe reflecting the clothing worn by other characters of your gender in the film or show. Cosplay is a safe space for gender expression of all kinds so feel free to reflect your own gender identity in your cosplays and your designs.

- The character might be a different skin colour to you; cosplaying a character who is a different race to you is not a problem, make and wear your costume because you love that character, just don't change your skin colour. There's no need, your costume is still awesome and you are still very much that character.
- You may want to make a design fit your height or body type better; the character you want to cosplay may be well over six feet and about the same width, so you can make changes to the costume to suit a different frame to the character, and still be imposing and feel powerful. No matter what you look like you should feel be able to embody the spirit of your chosen

character, and if that means making some changes in the design so that you do feel your very best self, go for it!

- You could change colours, patterns or design elements of the costume to something you think is better suited to a different version of the character; it may be that a character has a red costume in the film adaptation of a comic when their traditional colour in the comics is purple, and you may want to make their movie costume with comic book colours. It will look just as good with those different colours as a screen accurate version does and you'll have a version that is unique for you.

Galavant – *Galavant.*

You are allowed to make any changes you want and it will still be the character. It will be your version of the character, and that is what is important. You'll be your version. The thing that keeps coming back is that cosplay is an utterly personal experience. Your self-expression and self-exploration trump everything else as far as cosplay is concerned. The whole point of cosplay is that it is transformative. Not just transforming you into a character you love but transforming them into you and seeing that character as part of yourself. Which means no matter who you are you will always be the best version of that character, whether it's 100% accurate down to using the same zips that they had on the original costumes, or it's a completely new design out of your head. You made what you wanted to be. Brilliant!

Cosplay should help you feel positive in yourself, not feel bad or as if you have to change to be accepted into the community. No one should ever judge you for a costume not being 'accurate' because it doesn't matter.

There is a lot of joy in recreating things perfectly but just as much in adding your own changes and designing your own looks for a character. You don't need to feel controlled by accuracy or force yourself to make an 'accurate' costume at the expense of your own comfort or the comfort of others. Accuracy is not the be all and end all of cosplay.

With all this talk of designing a costume it might be a good idea to get making one.

Loki – Marvel Cinematic Universe.

SECTION 3

Making Cosplay and What Happens Next

Sewing – Fabric, Patterns and More

If you are a newcomer to sewing you'd be forgiven for thinking that all fabrics are basically the same when it comes to sewing a garment. That when using a sewing machine, you just zip your fabric of choice through no problem – but that is not the case. Each fabric has its own uses and properties. This means that some may be more suited for making hard wearing, heavy garments like coats or jeans, while others will

be better for a floaty summer dress or a romantic shirt. And you will have to sew each of these fabrics differently as well. Learning to recognise and handle your fabrics is a good starting point for anyone interested in making their costumes.

Plant-based fabrics

Plant-based fabrics, such as cotton or linen, are fabrics that can take a lot. They are strong and versatile, and won't be damaged by getting wet so can go through the wash (always a bonus as a cosplayer), can be ironed, steamed, dyed, embroidered, and painted. If you have a technique you want to try, plant-based fabrics are likely to be able to take it, and they'll probably be a-okay when you rip a seam open to resew it too.

- Cottons – Cottons are a group of great basic fabrics. They come in different weights, ranging from a lightweight dress-making cotton with floaty soft qualities, to a heavy cotton drill that is more suitable for overalls and uniforms. Cottons are made from natural fibres which means they will take dyes, though be careful of polycotton as it is a mix of cotton and man-made polyester so will not take dye properly. However, polycotton is cheaper than cotton and so can be used for cheap and cheerful builds or as lining. Every fabric has its uses. Cottons are very versatile and easy to use with basic sewing techniques, and can be used to create beautiful pieces as well as simple ones. One form of cotton that cosplayers use a lot of is calico. This is a rough and ready fabric that is perfect for making practice versions, known as toiles, of your garments. It's cheap, and comes in in so many different weights you'd be hard pressed not to find one that suits your needs and can take multiple uses as you get your garment fitted just right.
- Linen – Like cottons, linen is a natural fabric that comes in different weights and colours that can be put to multiple different uses. It is breathable and easy

to wear, but creases up the second you look away so be prepared to steam and iron this fabric a lot. This does mean though it will hold a crease well if you want one pressed into the fabric. Linen can be used to make suits, skirts, tops, bags, tablecloths, pillow cases, and more. It takes embroidery very well and can be used to make beautiful, rustic style garments for costumes.

- Other plant-based fabrics are: bamboo fibre, hemp, jute, ramie, sisal and soya bean fibre.

Right and previous page: Anne Bonny and Max – *Black Flag.*

Animal-derived fabric

While some animal-derived fabrics, such as fur, have fallen out of favour and seen as cruel, there are still fabrics in use that come from animals. Leathers, silks and wools all come from animals and all have their own unique properties that make them brilliant fabrics to use in your costumes.

Though they are often more expensive than plant-based fabrics, they make up for that in the properties they offer. Animal-derived fabrics are light in weight compared to the density of the fabric, have a natural elasticity and don't crease as much as plant based fabrics. They take dye just as well as plant-based fabrics too, but they aren't always as easy to wash and take care of, so make sure you look up washing instructions for the fabric you are using before sewing.

- Silk – It might come as a surprise to you but silk is the strongest natural fibre you can get. Made from the secretion of silkworms, silk is a fabric that has been connected with luxury and decadence for centuries. Depending on what the silkworms are fed you get different textures to the silk threads they create and thus different textures to the fabric. Because of this, silk can be used for a myriad of different garments from lightweight shirts and dresses to heavier suits and even coats. Silk can also be interwoven with other fabrics, natural and manmade, to make blends which can be cheaper than the real thing.
- Wool – Like silk, wools can have many different textures and weights; but unlike silk this is not to do with feeding sheep differently but instead to do with the different species of animal the wool comes from. Cashmere, alpaca, llama, and mohair all have their own unique feel compared to that of domestic sheep, some being much more expensive than others. Wool fabrics come in two types, woollen and worsted. Woollen fabrics are softer and fuzzier, and the less expensive of

the two types. They are bulky and warm, perfect for coats and jumpers. Worsted fabrics are stronger with a smooth texture and of a lighter weight. Examples of worsted fabrics would be gaberdine and twill suiting.

- Leather – Leather is somehow both an everyday fabric and a luxury one. With durability being one of the key properties of this material, leather is used for clothing, shoes, bags and upholstery. Quality leather is not the cheapest thing to get hold of in large quantities as you aren't buying a roll of woven fabric as you would with others, you going to be buying part or all of an animal hide. You can get off-cuts for making smaller accessories and items for not too much, and leather will only get better with age rather than having to worry about damage or it falling apart.

Man-made fabric

Man-made fabrics are pretty much what they say on the tin. Rather than being made from naturally derived fibres, this group of fabrics are made from fabrics that have been artificially created. This means that they come in a huge range of weird and wonderful textures, weights, weaves and colours. They can go beyond what a lot of natural fabrics can do, with more give and stretch, more ability to be shaped and hold that shape easily, and with cheaper processes in their creation so they can be a lot cheaper to buy.

Man-made fabrics are often an alternative to natural fabrics for either cost or ethical reasons. These fabrics include acrylic, elastane, nylon, polyester and vinyl.

- Acrylic – This is a man-made fabric that is used as an alternative to wool. You will see that fabric and knitting shops have a section of acrylic wools available, as people can be allergic to wool or they don't want to use animal products. You can get acrylic wool fabrics as well that are very durable and often used in upholstery.
- Elastane – Often known as spandex or by the brand name Lycra, elastane is stretch fabric used for sportswear and tightly fitted garments. It has a smooth finish and can be blended with fabrics like cotton to give stretch properties to different types of fabric. Elastane is very popular in fashion with styles like Athleisure wear rising on the high street. It's also perfect for making those tight fitting superhero costumes.
- Nylon – Nylon is one of the most versatile materials on the planet. It's not just a fabric, it's used in kitchen tools like spatulas, brush bristles, carpeting, ropes, and so much more. It's durable, versatile, and fibres of it will probably outlast the entire human race. When it comes to fabrics you'll probably know nylon tights, which are sheer and stretchy, though not at the same level of elastane, or you might have a raincoat made out of it. Nylon has so many uses and is a great fabric for sewing as it doesn't fray at the edges.
- Polyester – Like nylon, polyester is going to out-live us all. This fabric takes 20–200 years to biodegrade but it's one of the most used materials in the world due to its amazingly versatile qualities. Polyester is the base material for many fabrics that make up our modern wardrobes: polar fleece, velvet, microfibre fabrics and polyester blends can all be found on the high street. It can be used for and in almost everything.

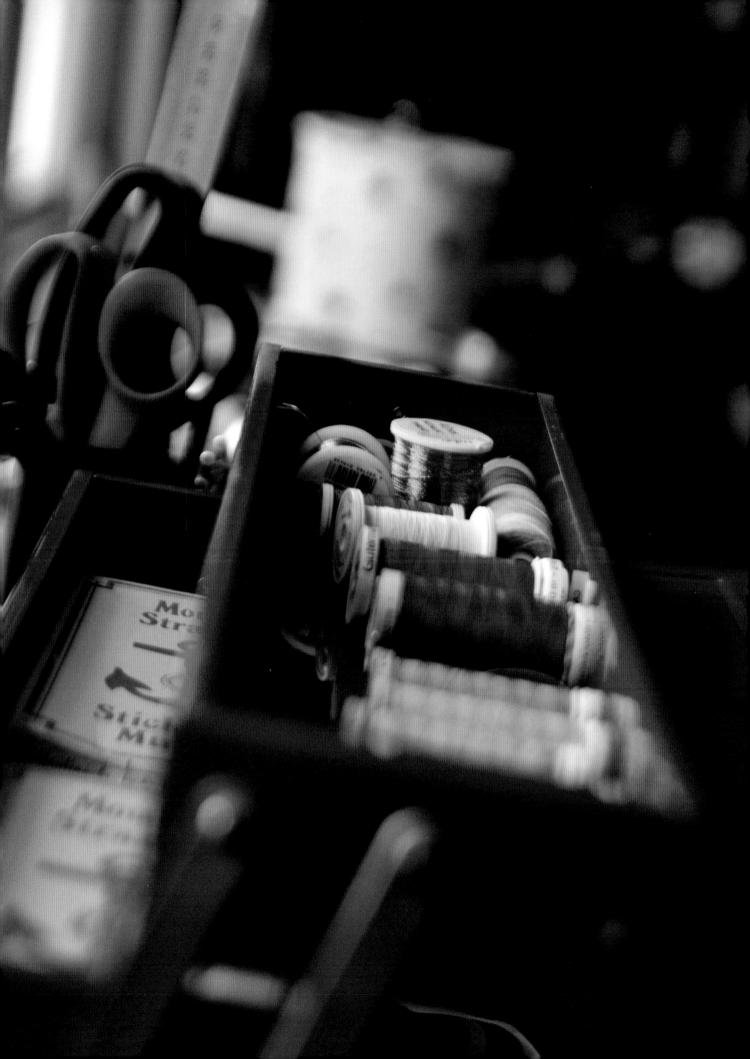

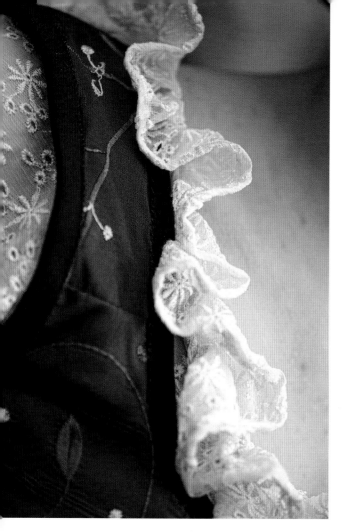

- Vinyl – Vinyl might summon up thoughts of LP records, but vinyl fabric is one of the more interesting man-made fabrics for making garments from. It is strong, waterproof and is mostly used for coats, bags and other outerwear. However, in alternative fashion circles vinyl has been used in much more exciting ways as it is not only strong but also creates bold shapes, as it is more like a sheet of plastic than more traditional fabrics. It can come in as many colours as you can think of, and even holographic and effervescent colouring can be made in vinyl. With similar qualities to leather, vinyl is often used as an animal-free substitute.

Looking at the weave

Most fabrics are woven. This means that they have threads that go vertically and horizontally, crossing over and under, to lock them together, and are made on a loom. The vertical is the warp and the horizontal is the weft. The warp is held stationary in the loom while the weft is taken from left to right, weaving through the threads of the warp. About half of the fabrics you will come across will have this plain style of weaving but some may be more open as there was less tension in the construction, while others will be very close. The differences in the weave give each fabric different properties that may or may not suit the garment you are making.

Tools you will need

Having the right tools for any job makes all the difference. When you're sewing you don't want to find you don't have the thing you need or that you break something that needs replacing.

- A sewing machine – A sewing machine doesn't need to be fancy, you can get to that later. Just make sure it works, you're happy using it and it does what you need. It's a good idea to make sure you have spare bobbins and needles when you start, and a few different types of sewing foot (button hole, zipper and a rolled hem foot are good starting points) for the machine.
- Good scissors – Get yourself a good pair of fabric and thread scissors. Don't skimp on scissors, they make all the difference. Keep them just for fabric and sewing. If anyone tries to use them for anything else you are allowed to cut off their fingers.
- Hand Sewing Needles – It is always useful to be able to hand stitch small things like fastenings and to close up seams.
- Pins – There are a whole range of pins available for different things but the best thing is to find what type works for you and your style of sewing rather than being dictated to by what the packaging says they are for.

- A Quick Unpick – We all make mistakes so it's good to have the tools to undo them. A quick unpick is a tool with a small, sharp hook that you can catch under stitches to pull them out carefully without damaging the garment.
- Tailor's Chalk – This comes in a few different forms, usually a pencil or flat disc, and is for marking your fabric with dots or lines without damaging it.

How to use patterns

Sewing clothes can be a touch daunting, thinking how are you going to get a fitted garment out of a flat piece of fabric, but never fear, a lot of people have come before you and have made instructions on exactly how to do that. These instructions are called patterns.

You can buy patterns in fabric shops and online from a range of different companies. In fabric shops they often have directories you can go through to find the pattern you need and it will have all the information about the fabric, fastenings and haberdashery you will need to create the garment.

Patterns range from easy sews all the way up to complex tailoring, so you can pick the ones that you feel happy making, or challenge yourself to the next level of sewing. A lot of pattern companies have started making patterns specifically for cosplay, so you can find Disney Princess, *Avengers*, *Game of Thrones* costumes and more as ready-to-use patterns. Some of these are even designed by cosplayers.

When you open up a pattern for the first time it might seem a little complex, but reading through the instructions, looking up terms you don't know and maybe having someone with a little more experience close at hand (sometimes this can be a book or Internet page) is the best way to muddle your way through. And don't panic if things go wrong, like sewing a seam the wrong way around or not fitting a sleeve properly. That's part of learning. You'll work out the problem, even if you have a cry first, and then you'll know what you did and remember not to do it next time.

You may also want to fit the costume to yourself better than a pre-made pattern will fit you, because pre-made is a bit like buying off the rack. One size does not fit all and you may have to make changes to the fit, so when you are sewing a garment it is worth making a practice version first, known as a toile, to make changes to the fit. You might find yourself doing this multiple times to get it perfect. You will need to do this as well if you are modifying a pattern.

You can also use patterns as a starting place for modifications into your own pattern ideas. Refitting in a different way, adding panels or seams, and sometimes changing the original pattern entirely and just using it as a base for fitting certain areas can mean that you end up with exactly the garment you want when you couldn't find a pre-made pattern for it. Some cosplays do have such odd designs, it's more than likely you'll find you have to modify a pattern at some point.

There are lots of ways of making patterns from scratch too. Draping fabric over a mannequin and pinning it to create shapes on which you can then mark the pattern

pieces you want is one way, or you can take your measurements and draw them up on pattern paper to create the pattern as a flat piece like any pattern you would buy. Making your own patterns can be trickier, but once you get your head round it, these methods are very useful for the weird and wonderful things cosplay throws at you. If you want to learn how to do this, courses on pattern drafting can be found at a lot of colleges, or some skilled seamers will offer private courses; there are also books and online tutorials you can use as a starting point.

Armour Making – Foam, Thermoplastics and Beyond

You could be tricked into thinking that cosplay armour is made from metal and you need a degree in smithing to make it. A lot of it can look very realistic, and in some cases you would be right, but mostly this is very much not the case. The armour that you see cosplayers wear is a very clever use of malleable foam sheets and thermoplastics.

There are other methods that are used, such as leather armour, cardboard and papier mâché, 3-D printing and, yes, metal work, but foam and thermoplastics tend to be the most popular amongst the cosplay community at present.

Foam

You must have seen craft foam sheets at some point, maybe at school or an art club, or you've used them in crafting projects at home. Colourful sheets of thin foam that cut easily and can be made into fun shapes, this is pretty much the same stuff that gets used to make cosplay armour and props, if you can believe it. Except the foam cosplayers use is on a much more epic scale.

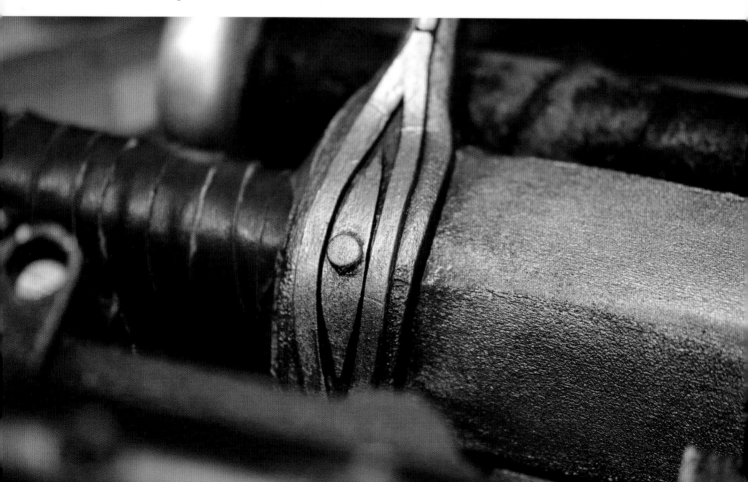

There are different types of foam that can be used for realistic looking armour and are frequently used because of their lightweight properties and ease of use. They require a heat gun to get the foam to give so it can be bent, glued into place, and then cooled in the desired position, without having to force it.

- EVA Foam – EVA stands for Ethylene Vinyl Acetate, which is a very sciencey term, but to a cosplayer this means that this is the most dense and resistant type of foam. EVA foam comes in a variety of thicknesses depending on what you need it for. It is easy to cut and shape with the use of a heat gun. Foam has less give than a thermoplastic and you will find that you need to have darts and tailoring techniques to create more dramatic shapes in a similar way to fabric garment construction. EVA foam can be secured along seams with contact glues and will be incredibly sturdy when finished. It also doesn't require sanding, having a smooth texture even after being heated, which is always a bonus. The sheets of foam you can get range in weight and size and you can get them on most cosplay crafting sites, such as Poly Props.
- Craft Foam – Yes the stuff kids use. It's basically the same as EVA foam but thinner and therefore easier to shape. It can be great for making things like spikes or 3-D decorative elements on armour that won't need to take any weight or strain, as well as flat designs, insignias or other patterns on the surface of the armour or prop that want a little more depth than just being painted on.
- Foam Clay – This is a new material on the cosplay scene but is definitely finding its place amongst foam users. A mouldable clay that air dries and takes on the form of foam when set; it's pretty amazing! You can shape it into anything, sculpt it into pieces of detail like faces or animals, press it into moulds to make scrolling

patterns, or form it into gems, and it's great for filling in any cracks in seams or elsewhere on a costume and then sanding it down smooth as if it were never there.

If you want to learn to use foam, Evil Ted and Punished Props websites and YouTube channels are good starting points.

Thermoplastics

Thermoplastics are a magic invention that has really taken off in the cosplay scene. You may remember seeing or using a vacuum former with heated plastic at school, and thermoplastics are a similar idea: sheets that you can heat and mould into the shapes you want. Fortunately, they do not require a vacuum former and that level of heat to make them work. Some can be shaped with hot water, some with a heat gun or a hair dryer.

- Worbla – Worbla comes in large sheets in regular (a sort of brown colour), black and clear; it has a slight texture to it, not dissimilar to sandpaper, and can be heated with a heat gun or hair dryer to mould into shapes. Unlike foam, Worbla can be heated to a point where you can literally roll it up into a ball and flatten it back out again. When hot it is almost like clay. It sticks to itself so doesn't require glue, but because it is so malleable it can become floppy and stick to itself at the wrong time and be damaged, or get air bubbles in it as it's heated. It's also trickier to handle and to avoid deforming the shape you want. Because of its texture it does need sanding to get a smooth finish. However, it can be made into almost anything from armour to lenses, prop weapons to gem stones, and you can even put lights and LEDs into it with minimal effort. The sheets come in various different sizes and are available on most cosplay websites.
- Thermocraft – Similar to Worbla but smoother and with a more seamless finish when stuck together, Thermocraft is still relatively new to the scene but is becoming popular amongst armour and props builders. It doesn't need as much sanding, but is tricky to use in larger pieces, as when it sticks to itself you might as well scrap it.
- Polymorph Beads – This thermoplastic comes in the form of small beads, as the name suggests, instead of a sheet like the others. You submerge the beads in a bowl of boiling water and leave them to get soft in the heat. This can take a few minutes but once they are warm and malleable they are great for shaping into small props or details for larger pieces. Cosplayers use them to make things like wands, decorative beads, blades for fake swords and knives, arrow heads and fake fangs (though very carefully in this case, as you don't want to burn your mouth!)

Other materials for armour making

It's not all foam and plastic work in armour building. There are some more 'old school' skills being used to create armour pieces too. Traditional methods like leatherwork and

smithing turn up more frequently than you would think, and it's wonderful to keep those crafts alive. Both of these can be learned from master crafts people, as courses in traditional crafts are becoming more and more popular around the country. If you have a look in your local area you may be surprised to find someone running a class that you could go along to.

There is also the ever overlooked carboard and papier mâché armour build. It's cheap, easy (we've all had a go at it at some point or another), can be carefully sanded and smoothed out like thermoplastics, and waterproofed at a pinch. It does take more time as you have to wait for layers to dry but cardboard can be used the same as foam, with glue and tape to connect the seams and you can even use the same patterns that you would use for foam or thermoplastic builds. Plus you're doing a bit to save the planet, recycling old cardboard boxes and newspaper!

Tools

- Heat Gun – A heat gun is a device for rapidly heating up a surface or object. Though they look similar to a hair dryer they get much hotter; some can even get up 500°c. If the heat is a worry for you a hair dryer will work but is much slower. You can get heat guns in most DIY shops.
- Craft Knife – A sharp craft knife is a foam user's best friend. It's easier to cut out fiddly patterns in thick foam with a craft knife than a pair of scissors. You can

get a couple of different types so it is worth testing a few out to see which one suits you best.

- Scissors – You always need scissors. But make sure you mark your fabric scissors and your foam/thermoplastic scissors as different! You don't want to mix them up.
- Sandpaper – No matter if you use foam, thermoplastic or paper mâché you are going to need to sand down your project at some point. Having a few different grades (roughness) of sandpaper will make your finished project smoother and more precise looking.
- Dremel – This is a handheld power tool for sanding with. It has a small head with sandpaper on that spins incredibly fast and can sand down edges much quicker than just doing it by hand. You can get them in DIY shops as well.
- Glues – There are loads of different glues to choose from, but most foam users will recommend contact glues for a firm hold.
- Applicators – If you are using glue, you don't want to put it on with your fingers!
- Goggles, masks and gloves – A lot of the things you use for foam work can be dangerous, so you want to protect yourself. Using any type of power tool, sanding equipment, knives or glues, you could breathe in something nasty, cut yourself or get grit, foam/plastic dust, or a broken piece of a Dremel in your eye. Nasty! Best to look after yourself.
- Space – Not really a tool, but working with glues and power tools you need to have a good, clear space where you can work safely. Working in a garage, shed or outside is best, if you can.

Patterns

Like fabric, you need patterns to do an armour build. While these aren't so readily available in shops, you can get your hands on a myriad of different patterns online and there are books made by cosplayers that not only have patterns but include clear instructions on how to use them.

As with fabric patterns you can modify the ones you get for armour so that they suit your needs and design ideas better, but it's worth practicing with a basic one and following the instructions first so you know what you are doing. Foam can be quite expensive and you don't want to cut it wrong and make a mistake. Making the pattern in paper or thin card before you make it in foam will make a real difference to making sure your final version is as good a possible. You can adjust the card version and make it multiple times to make sure you are completely happy before transferring your final version to foam.

If you want to make sure your armour pieces fit you well, doing these tests is a must, especially for pieces that go around any part of the body rather than just sitting on your shoulders. If it doesn't fit right it could fall off or break from being too tight, or just be uncomfortable to wear all day. So test and modify all your pattern pieces to get the right size for you before you start your build in your final materials.

You can also make your own patterns. Though you can't drape like you can with fabric, you can make your own patterns on a mannequin or your own body with just

some plastic wrap and masking tape. Wrap the plastic around the area of your body or mannequin that you want to make the pattern for, then cover it in masking tape, building up any areas you want to be more shaped or exaggerated with newspaper taped into place. Then use a marker pen to draw on the shape of your pattern and cut it off. Lie the piece flat and see if any darts or seams are needed to create the final shape you want.

If you are interested in learning to use or make patterns for foam, Evil Ted, Punished Props and Kamui Cosplay are the best places to start. Contact information is in the References section at the end of this book.

Priming, painting and finishing

Foams, thermoplastics, or papier mâché don't come with the perfect finished look; it takes a bit more work to get them to look right for your final costume. They will have seam lines or texture to them that you don't want to be seen, so you have to know how to finish everything off.

The impulse is to start painting your armour straight away but these materials are thirsty and will drink that paint straight up so you'll end up doing layers and layers to get a basic coating. Instead use a few layers of primer on your armour to stop that happening, and by happy coincidence show up any areas that still need a little sanding or filling in with foam clay or acrylic fillers to smooth them off properly. You will definitely find yourself doing a sand, prime, fill, repeat cycle at least once per armour build no matter what. Just a fact of cosplay.

Cosplayers use a few different types of primer: spray primer which you can get in DIY shops, car/bike repair shops or art shops as well as specialist cosplay shops online, or a paint-on primer called gesso. Gesso can be bought in art shops as it is used for priming canvas before paint. Spray primers have the benefit of not leaving brush lines that need to be buffed or sanded out, and do dry quickly, but are more expensive. Gesso goes a long way, is cheaper for more of it, and you can make it yourself if you really want to but you have to put in more time for it to dry and to get it smooth.

Once you're happy with your surface, it's smooth, primed and ready to paint.

Really basic acrylic paint will do just fine for painting your armour. You can get that on with brushes, sponges, pieces of cloth, scrunched up paper, whatever you want to get the texture and feel that looks right for your build. You can get acrylics

in most art or craft shops and it comes in big tubs and tubes so you can get through a lot of armour before it runs out. You can also water it down to get different levels of coverage in different areas of the armour, which is great for weathering or detailing effects on your costume.

If you fancy a smoother finish, spray paints or an air brush will help you get that. Like spray primer this is the pricier option but spray paints give a really clean look to a project, and you may want to go with acrylic afterwards to add details that can't be done with a spray.

An air brush is a bit of an investment when you start cosplaying, but if you find you really like making armour and props, you might want to look into getting one later down the line. An air brush gives you the smooth spray finish of a spray paint but with much more control as you can change the size of area being sprayed, the strength of the spray and the intensity of the paint colour. It's a very versatile piece of kit.

Whatever way you decide to paint your costume do remember to finish it with a good spray or paint-on varnish as you don't want all that hard work to get ruined in the rain! A varnish finish can be shiny, gloss or matt depending on the type you get, so read the label to get the right one for your project.

Buying, Commissioning and Modifying

You don't have to be a master craftsperson to dip your toes into the ocean of cosplay. Seeing all the things you need to learn and buy to get started with crafting your own costumes, while exciting to some, is a bit off-putting to others. Thankfully, with the huge rise in cosplay's popularity as a hobby you can now buy high quality, pre-made costumes and costume pieces.

While it's always fun to try your hand at crafting, and there is something to be said for being able to point to something you have made, it isn't always for all the cosplayers, all the time. Being able to order a costume and just put it on straight away is a great way to get involved in the hobby, and not having to stress about every part of every costume is much more relaxing.

There are several different options beyond buying a costume off the Internet's version of the rack, each with its own pros and cons to consider if you want to take this route.

Premade costumes

There has, in the last five or so years, appeared a large amount of cosplay shops and sellers, providing costumes for cosplayers that can be made to measure (to a greater or lesser extent) or bought in a range of sizes, not dissimilar to picking a pair of jeans in a high street store.

Kaylee – *Firefly*.

While not cheap as chips, these costumes are normally good quality for a price that won't break the bank. Obviously the more you spend the more likely you are to get a higher quality product, but make sure you check the reviews and ask other cosplayers if they have bought from the shop or seller before, as some can be scams or using stolen images to sell products that look nothing like them.

If you are looking to buy a pre-made costume, Cosplay Sky, EZ Cosplay, ProCosplay and Xcoser should be your first points of call. All have high ratings, good quality costumes and a wide range of items to pick from.

It is also a good idea to find a local dressmaker, alteration or sewing repair shop. If you want to make sure that your costume fits perfectly but aren't too keen on trying to do the fitting yourself, taking it along to your local alternation shop will mean that, for just a little more cost, your costume will fit like a glove.

Anna and Elsa –
Frozen.

There is also the option of buying a costume that another cosplayer has already made. Every so often cosplayers like to have a clear out and so will sell on old costumes to a new home. This is will be advertised on their social media of choice. If you see someone selling a costume of theirs you like, jump in there and get it! You'll be giving that costume a new lease of life.

Kristoff, Anna, Elsa, Hans and Oaken – Frozen.

Commissioning a costume

If you have more cash to splash, you can always get a costume commissioned.

A lot of cosplayers and costume makers offer commissions, many doing it as their business. You'll know a cosplayer who offers commissions because they will say it's their livelihood; so they will be advertising it loud and proud, be it on their Etsy, Facebook, Instagram or Twitter pages, and they will let people know if commissions are open or closed. This is so anyone interested can get put on the list or take an available slot in the maker's time table.

Most will be happy to chat with you and give you a quote for a piece, but be aware that this is their business, so don't try and haggle or mess them around if you can't afford their prices. These are skilled individuals running a business, they are offering the price that they know will not just cover costs of materials but also their time and

Deet – *The Dark Crystal.*

Oaken – *Frozen.*

make them a profit. If they offer a quote you can't afford they will be fine if you just tell them that up front and thank them for their time. And be honest, if you need to take some time to think about it and get back to them, just don't leave it too long as they may lose out on other business. Respect goes a long way.

The joy of a commissioned piece is that you will get exactly what you want. You can talk design, fabric choices, accessories, add-ons and more, as well as it being made to your measurements, so you have all the choices to make it perfect. Commissioned cosplays are normally higher quality than premade, store bought ones since they aren't mass produced, so you will find that things like pattern matching fabric, using high quality materials across the board and having an overall cleaner finish are present. Cosplay makers take pride in their work so by buying from them you are supporting a small business with higher standards than a mass produced factory piece.

Again, always check the reviews. You don't want to waste your money on a scam.

Buying and Modifying Clothing

Making cosplay out of the everyday is a joy. Really it is. Digging around in a charity shop, hunting through eBay, or seeing an accurate piece in a shop window can make a cosplayer's day. If you can upcycle something you found for £2 in a second hand shop into the perfect jacket for your Black Widow costume just by dyeing it a different colour or adding a collar and buttons, go for it! You don't need to scratch build everything, nor to have to buy a perfect pre-made replica: this is a half way house.

Sewing patches, adding painted designs or embroidery to a shirt, gluing armour sections or any sort of unusual additions to some dungarees, refitting a coat to look more like the character; there is so much you can do to modify pre-existing garments and turn them into costume pieces. And it doesn't need to be just clothing either, plenty of household items could find a second life as a cosplay prop. Captain America's shield? Make it out of a bin lid. A wizard's wand? The handle of a paint brush or an old chopstick painted and embellished with gems, sparkles and a crafting magic. You don't need to be restricted by 'official' crafting materials. If you think it will work and do the job you want, give it a go!

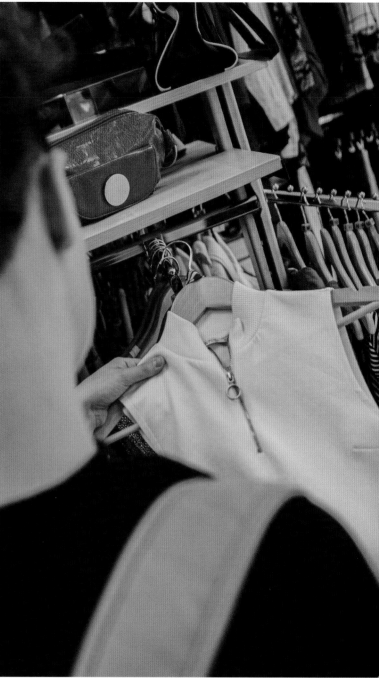

It doesn't need to be changing these pieces completely either. Some characters wear 'standard' clothing so there's not that much point in making their items from scratch. If you can buy something similar, buy it. You can always change buttons or sew a ribbon on if it needs it. A lot of these 'everyday' costume pieces come from fashion brands, maybe not the cheapest ones, but replica or screen-accurate costumes from films or TV shows can be found in high street stores if you keep an eye out. Fans of the shows or films you are looking for pieces from sometimes have groups or social media pages with information about where to buy from so you don't need to do the hard work on that front!

Bella Swan – *The Twilight Saga.*

Conventions – What Should you Expect?

Golly! It's that time already! Your costume is finished and you just can't wait to show it off, but how to do that, eh? You've already thrown it up on all your social media pages, so it's about time you got your skates on and headed to a comic con, or convention, and strutted your stuff in the big, wide, real world of cosplay.

There's this idea with going to your first convention that you need to jump in the deep end and get the 'whole experience', but there is more than one way to skin a cat, as they say. Finding your feet with conventions so that you actually enjoy the experience is important, and understanding what you want to get out of these events will make all the difference to your convention 'career' as it were.

For a lot of newcomers to the nerd scene the image they have of conventions is the huge, global events like San Diego, New York or London Comic Cons. These are the peak of what conventions can be and they are as huge as they seem in the pictures. Your first time at any of these large-scale events can be overwhelming to even the seasoned convention goer; there really is nothing like San Diego Comic Con. For anyone with social anxiety issues or who might be a bit shy, throwing yourself into these types of events headfirst just might be a step too far. If you are new to cosplay

and conventions it might be worth considering other events before you jet off to London or further afield.

In the last 10 years, while the big conventions have gotten bigger, many smaller, local events have sprung up in their wake. It's easy now to find a convention just down the road from you at some point in the year that won't be on the scale of the big, central shows. These local events can range from being a slightly smaller version of the London conventions, held in other major cities, right the way down to a village hall celebrating with a one-day event that is basically a nerd summer fête. It's kind of wonderful.

With these smaller, local events you are more likely to find a friendlier, more welcoming environment across the board. This isn't to say that larger ones aren't inclusive, but with so many people there it can be tricky to make new connections if you are someone who's a little shy. People will welcome you into the community wherever you go in cosplay, but at these smaller events, it's a lot less intimidating and it's more than likely these cosplayers are from your area, so you can make friends, or even when you do feel ready to go to a bigger show you have people to go with. There is more of a feeling of 'the convention family' ready to take new cosplayers under their wing.

Smaller events are also a great place to test drive your costumes in a more relaxed and social atmosphere. Knowing that your armour isn't going to fall apart on you, and this happens even to the most experienced cosplayers every now and then, is incredibly helpful no matter where you are in your cosplay journey. You will want to know what works, and what doesn't for a long day in costume when you're wearing something new.

John Rambo – *Rambo.*

Whatever event you go to there are two things to remember before you go.

Firstly, all conventions and events no matter the size, will have costume and prop safety guidelines. Events will often say 'family friendly' and that will be reflected in their costume guides.

Conventions may well ask cosplayers not to bring realistic weapons, wear make-up with excessive gore, or wear costumes that could be seen as overtly sexual. Every convention has its own costume guidelines, so check the website or event page so you know what's what. You don't want to find you can't go in or have your hard work taken off you at the door just because you didn't check!

Secondly, you should always remember to bring cash with you. Decide your budget for the weekend and bring that in cash or visit a cash point outside of the venue at the start of the day. Queues at cash points in the convention can be long and often the machines can run out altogether, if there even is a cash point at all. While it is becoming more common for vendors and food stands at conventions to have card readers, it is not always the case and you have no idea how annoying it is when you want to buy that cute pin you've had your eye on all day and you're completely out of cash.

Budgeting is an important part of cosplay and convention-going, not just for the costume and the convention ticket but for everything else around it. It's worth planning out your costs before you start spending so you know what you can afford with your costume, tickets, purchases on the day and hotel and travel costs.

Hotels and travel

Outside of the cosplays themselves, hotels and travel are pretty much always going to be the biggest expense any cosplayer has.

When considering going to a convention, the price of your accommodation and travel needs to be at the top of your mind, even above the price of the tickets. A lot of the hotels near big venues will put their prices up if they know that an event is happening, so keep an eye out for deals and advanced booking to try and cut the price. If you're going in a group, try and get a hotel together. It cuts costs and it's nice to have that social side to your weekend built in, but don't try to cheat the system. It might seem clever but over-filling a room is never the way to go. Hotels have these rules for a reason and you don't want to lose your room to save a few pounds.

If you want to try and save some more money, and don't mind travelling in the mornings, you could look for a hotel a little further away from the venue or rent an apartment that you can share with more people. Apartments are, in actual fact, a great option. Not only can they work out cheaper overall but you can also save a little money on food and drink because you're likely to have a kitchen and be able to make up food packs for the day and cook meals in the evening, rather than having to eat out on top of all the other costs. Plus this is a super-cute group bonding activity for all your cosplay buddies.

As for travel, it's pretty much common sense. When it comes to using public transport to get to an event, booking trains and coaches in advance to get the best price is a must. And keeping an eye on works, strikes or any other issues that might cause a problem with your travel will make your life a little easier too. Don't get caught out with all the trains being cancelled and no way to get anywhere.

Public transport can be a bit of an issue for costumes whether you are wearing them to the convention or carrying them, so this is something to consider if you are staying a little way from the venue or are just going for the day. If your costume involves larger pieces like wings, armour or large weapons, it's best to package them up safely and securely with a big 'FRAGILE' sticker attached so people are aware, and give you some

Falcon – Marvel Cinematic Universe.

room to keep your things safe. If you have weaponry of any sort keep it packaged up in a box, or a bag, or wrapped up and well secured, as you can get in trouble carrying a weapon in public, even if it's convention safe.

If you are at all worried about being in your costume in public, wearing a coat, jumpsuit or onesie over the top of it can save you from awkward situations with strangers and keep your hard work safe from any risk of damage while in transit. But make sure the venue has a cloakroom available because there's nothing more annoying than finding out you're going to have to lug your things around with you all day! If there isn't a designated cloakroom, see if any friends are staying closer to the venue so you can store your stuff with them and go on to enjoy your day unimpeded.

You can also contact the event ahead of time to see if a cloakroom or designated changing space is, or can be made, available to cosplayers. Most conventions want to do the best they can for their attendees and will try to accommodate these needs if they can.

Travelling to a convention is never easy. You have a lot of stuff and even if you drive, you can be piled high with wigs, props, costumes and more, squishing everyone into their seats. Taking some measures to make your time at the event easier before you get there is worth the effort, since you've already put so much into your cosplays.

Planning your day

Planning your day/weekend at a comic con is more important than you might think. Knowing what you want to do and see will help you get the best out of your time there.

Conventions spend months before the main event releasing the names of guests, planning panel times and creating a programme of events that will appeal to a multitude of different people. Having a look online to see what is going on means that you can see what you're interested in and how you want to spend your time. A lot of conventions now have specialised apps so you can see the whole weekend of programming and mark up what you would like to do. This is especially helpful if there are last minute cancellations of guests and their panels, so you can rethink your day without stress if something you wanted to do is no longer happening.

If you want to get more information about cosplay at an event, sign up for the competition or want to chat to a cosplay guest, most events now have a dedicated cosplay zone full of interesting cosplayers to talk to about the hobby and give advice. There will also be a cosplay repair station of some sort, which is everyone's best friend at one point or another.

However try not to go overboard as you'll end up rushing from one thing to the next, missing out that special sort of serendipity that conventions have, but having a few waypoints during the day when you know you will be doing a certain thing helps give you a structure to work around.

If it's your first time going to a convention in cosplay, maybe look out for any cosplay or fandom meets that you would like to attend. These are a great way to make friends and to meet other cosplayers who are in the same fandoms as you. Meets are the perfect place to share your love for cosplay and fandom, get tips on making costumes and maybe even find inspiration for your next build. On top of that it's an opportunity to take pictures with people and of your costume after all your hard work.

If this is all a bit too much for you, you can simply chat and exchange social media pages rather than hang around for longer than you feel comfortable with, or you can bring along a friend.

The best way to find out about meets is to join some online cosplay groups or communities as most will arrange meets for cons. Being in a mixture of local and country-wide groups, as well as ones for different fandoms, will give you a variation on meets that are available to you, so you'll always have some friendly faces to find at an event.

Enfys Nest – *Solo: A Star Wars Story*.

Din Djarin and Grogu – *The Mandalorian*.

Cosplay is not Consent

In the age of the #metoo movement and the ban on 'upskirting', cosplayers have their own movement to help protect each other against sexual harassment or any other type of persecution on the convention floor or online. It is called 'Cosplay is Not Consent' and it is both a movement and a mantra.

No matter what, cosplayers are not inviting you into their space just because they are dressed as your favourite character. Be respectful of cosplayers, even if you are in costume yourself; do not touch them, take photographs of them without their permission, follow them, make unkind or derogatory comments in person or online about them, knowingly misgender them in anyway (especially if you have been corrected), or make comments on their shape, size, gender, sexuality, race or religious identity. Cosplay does not mean that a cosplayer is fair game to be upset, hurt or worse.

Almost all conventions now have an enforced 'Cosplay is Not Consent' policy to keep cosplayers safe from anyone who might want to take advantage or be unpleasant in any way. This means that people have been removed from conventions due to their behaviour, had complete bans on attending again, and have even been reported to the police. Conventions want to keep everyone safe so everyone has a good time.

The cosplay zone at conventions will normally have an anti-bullying policy as well, so you can go there to inform people of anything that has

Granny Weatherwax – *Terry Patchett's Discworld.*

made you feel uncomfortable if you don't want to go directly to a convention staff member. The cosplay organisers are always there to help out.

Unfortunately, these types of things are harder to police online. But the community has made a great effort to look after each other, creating online safe spaces, such as She-Props, and the UK Cosplay Community, as well as always being on the ball to report accounts and users across social media who try to troll cosplayers.

Self-care in Cosplay

There's a little phrase in cosplay that every cosplayer knows and fears: con-crunch. This is when you are pushing yourself to finish a costume for your next big convention and the costume build takes over your whole life. Pulling all-nighters for days on end, sewing on the train or in the car on the way to the convention and even finishing things in the hotel room the morning of the event are a cosplayer's worst nightmare, and all of us have lived it at some point. There's a lot of pressure on cosplayers, especially felt by newcomers to the hobby, to always have something new and to push yourself to finish things for the next event rather than enjoying the process and not stressing out unduly over a project. It's time we learnt some self-care.

When it comes to cosplay, your physical, mental and emotional health should always be your priority. Convention in a week and you haven't finished (or possibly haven't started) a new costume? Weigh up your options instead of charging full-on into a stressful week of sleepless nights and hand cramp. Can you finish this costume in time? Do you have another costume you could wear if you don't think you can? Do you have friends who could help out or lend you the parts you are missing, or the whole costume? Are you feeling up to doing such a large amount of work in the time, physically and mentally? And most of all, will it be worth the stress?

Often you will have more fun if you take a moment to breathe, put the unfinished build to one side and wear something else. If you do have friends who can help you out by lending you the parts that are missing, reach out and ask rather than trying to make it all in a small amount of time, and give yourself the time and space to work on your costume in the future.

Sometimes making a costume fast can be really fun, but so can taking it slow, so make sure you think about what will be best for you in the situation. Con-template before you con-crunch (yes, I will see myself out).

Speaking of conventions, you can't go wrong with a bit of self-care at an event. Building time into your schedule for self-care for both your costume build and your convention plans is never going to be a bad idea.

An Orc – *The Lord of the Rings*.

There are plenty of things that can go wrong if you push yourself to wear a costume for too long at an event.

Knowing how long you plan on spending in your costume and when to take breaks from wearing it is important. If you need to get changed, get changed. Don't overdo it because you feel as if you've put time and money into a costume, you can always wear it again. You will have a better experience putting yourself above your cosplay, and wearing something multiple times means you get more chances to improve your costume; it could be a chance to make it more comfortable so you can wear it for longer in the future.

No matter what your costume is like, make some time to sit and relax during the day and get out of it if you can. It will make you feel a lot better to rest up and you'll be more likely to enjoy your day and your costume.

After a long time on your feet in a costume that may not be hugely comfortable, you don't want to get back to your hotel and not have everything you need to get yourself going again. Taking a self-care kit to a convention is a must: plasters, pain-killers and muscle gels/rubs for during and after a convention are never a bad thing. No matter how broken-in your shoes are, or how well you built your armour harness, there can always be problems with comfort. You will want to be able to take care of a rubbed foot or an aching back as soon as possible so it doesn't ruin the rest of your day.

Getting dehydrated can be easily done. Cosplays can be hot and convention centres can be hotter; not making time to eat or drink enough is a common mistake for cosplayers old and new alike. Bring some food and water with you, replenishing on the go between panels is better than not doing it at all, and it's a good excuse to craft yourself a bag to match your costume. Like cosplayers need more excuses to craft! Or include some good sized pouches or pockets to carry snacks. I'm pretty sure Batman has a snack pouch in that utility belt of his. There's no harm in having a stash of some easy to eat snacks in your hotel room, and stock up on tea, coffee, or soft drinks, so you can replenish your energy stores as soon as you free yourself from your costume. Breakfast bars and crisps are the cosplayer's usual snack food of choice

But self-care doesn't end when you take the costume off. A shower or a bath at the end of the day at a convention is one of the great joys of cosplaying. Weirdly. Soaking your muscles, getting that body paint off and giving your hair a good wash after it's been under a wig give you time to appreciate all of the good things about cosplay while you wash away any of the discomfort and tiredness. It makes you feel human again, or as close as possible at a convention anyway.

It's easy to fall into the trap of not looking after yourself in favour of getting things finished 'on time' or doing all the different photoshoots and meets at a convention. You don't want to miss out. But if you set good habits early with how you make your costumes, how you go about wearing them and looking after yourself and your friends at conventions, and being able to take a breath and step away from it all if you need a break, you'll find your own rhythm and enjoyment in the hobby rather than being swept along by peer pressure.

Be kind to yourself, it's only dressing up.

Greta Gremlin and Gizmo – *Gremlins*.

Rapunzel – *Tangled*.

Little Extras

A few things to think about when wearing cosplay for the first time:

What are you wearing under it?

This probably sounds silly but knowing what is under your costume is as important as the costume itself. If you are wearing something tight on the downstairs it's polite for people of all genders to wear underwear that will not only protect them from embarrassing pictures but also won't upset the public at large. Dance belts are perfect for wearing with that Superman costume as they are developed for male dancers to make sure that no accidents happen mid-leap during *Swan Lake*. You can also look into shape wear underwear or dance tights. This isn't exactly to change your shape but more to make sure that everything is held in place, and fabric like Lycra skims over anything you might not want on show. No one wants to see pictures online afterwards with an unfortunate camel toe, now do they?

If you do want to change up your body shape in any way then more extreme types of shapewear like compression under armour, waist trainers, corsets, padded bras, pants or tights, and chest binders are all easy to get hold of but make sure you don't over do it with anything too tight. Always look up instructions and tutorials with corsets, binders and compression wear so you know how to wear them safely. The drag community have wonderful advice on all of these things and more for changing up your shape, as do historical re-enactors, for two different ways at looking at the same topic.

Who are you going with?

Having a buddy system at a convention is a must! They are big and full of people, so knowing who you are with and where you are meeting them is important. If you get separated have a pre-arranged meeting point where you can find each other, as often phone signal is non-existent due to the sheer volume of people at the event.

Write important phone numbers on your arm or leg. This will mean that even if your phone dies while you are on your own you can ask to borrow one from staff and find your people. This is especially important if you are going it alone or meeting friends when you get there. You don't want to be stranded.

Find a safe space that won't move, as you never know when you might need a friendly face. This can be the cosplay desk, or a friend who has a table in the vendors' area. People move around a lot so you can't always rely on your friends being where you left them, and knowing you can go somewhere if things go wrong and people will look after you is important to making sure your day won't get ruined by something silly.

Don't worry

Stuff happens. Costumes break. Your train runs late. You get stuck in traffic. It's not the end of the world.

If you are worried about your costume, bring a small repair kit with you that can fit in your bag. If you're worried about public transport for whatever reason, make a plan for your travel and have a back-up route if anything goes wrong, but sometimes you can't control it if there are works on the line or a bus doesn't show up. The same for driving.

It's not fun when things go wrong but if nothing else it can be your funny story for the weekend. Take it in your stride as best you can, you got this.

Right and opposite:
Moana – *Moana.*

References and Further Reading

Section 1: What is Cosplay?

What is Cosplay? Looking into the Hobby

Ashcraft, B. and Plunkett, L., 2014. *Cosplay World*. New York: Munich.

Crawford, G. and Hancock, D., 2019. *Cosplay And The Art Of Play*. 1st ed. Palgrave Macmillan.

Culp, J., 2016. *Cosplay*. Rosen Publishing Group, Inc.

MacCarthy, H., 2014. *A Brief History Of Manga*. Lewes: Ilex.

Cohaku, The Cosplay Magazine, English Editions, Issues 1–5, https://www.cohaku.de/cohaku01-english/

The Cosplay Journal, Volumes 1–5, www.thecosplayjournal.com

Helen McCarthy, writer and historian, https://helenmccarthy.wordpress.com/

Sarkar, P., 2020. *History Of Cosplay*. [online] Vocal. Available at: https://vocal.media/geeks/history-of-cosplay

History of Cosplay

Pre-1900

Johnson, J H., 2011. *Venice incognito: masks in the Serene Republic*, Berkeley: University of California Press.

Oakley, M., 2019. History of Costume: Carnivals, cosplay, kings and the anonymity of costume. *The Cosplay Journal*, (3), p.38.

Gentle Author., n.d. A Wedding Dress Of Spitalfields Silk. *Spitalfields Life*. Saltyard Book Co., 2013. [online]: https://spitalfieldslife.com/2011/04/29/a-wedding-dress-of-spitalfields-silk/

1900–1950s

Storey, J., 2007. *Cultural Theory And Popular Culture*. Harlow: Pearson Prentice Hall.

Millar, R., 2020. *Was Mr. Skygack The First Alien Character In Comics?*. [online] io9. Available at: https://io9.gizmodo.com/was-mr-skygack-the-first-alien-character-in-comics-453576089

Hansen, R., 2020. *COSPLAY: 1930s to 1950s*. [online] Fiawol.org.uk

Fancyclopedia.org. 2020. *Morojo - Fancyclopedia 3*. [online] Available at: http://fancyclopedia.org/Morojo

Racked. 2020. *Meet The Woman Who Invented Cosplay*. [online] Available at: https://www.racked.com/2016/5/9/11451408/cosplay-inventor-morojo-myrtle-r-douglas

1960–1990s

Duncan, R. and Smith, M., n.d. *The Power Of Comics*.

Ditko, S., n.d. *The 1964 New York Comicon*. 1st ed. Totalmojo Productions, Incorporated.

Howe, S., n.d. *Marvel Comics*. 1st ed. Harper Perennial.

Morrison, G., 2012. *Supergods*. New York: Spiegel & Grau.

Kaminski, M., 2008. *The Secret History Of Star Wars*. Kingston, Ont.: Legacy Books Press.

2000 to Present

Winge, T., n.d. *Costuming Cosplay*. 1st ed. Bloomsbury Visual Arts.

Phelan, E., 2020. *Cosplay: A 21st Century Form Of Escapism*. [online] Medium. Available at: https://medium.com/@EdwardPhelan1/cosplay-a-21st-century-form-of-escapism-2f8ea84f9c81

Moore, J., n.d. *Street Style In America*. Greenwood.

Chuang, E., Letamendi, A., Ohanesian, L. and Shikarius, n.d. *Cosplay In America V2*.

Different Types of Costuming – An Intersectional Subculture

Moore, F., 1994. *Drag!* Jefferson (N.C.): McFarland.

Schacht, S., 2004. *The Drag Queen Anthology*. New York, N.Y., London: Harrington Park Press.

The Nation. 2020. *The First Drag Queen Was A Former Slave*. [online] Available at: https://www.thenation.com/article/society/drag-queen-slave-ball/

Simkins, D., n.d. *The Arts Of LARP*.

Roth, S., 2000. *Past Into Present*. [United States]: The University of North Carolina Press.

Moore, T., 2008. *I Believe In Yesterday*. London: Cape.

Robb, B., n.d. *Steampunk*. 1st ed. Voyageur Press.

Vandermeere, J. and Chambers, S., 2011. *The Steampunk Bible*. New York: Abrams.

Le Zotte, J., n.d. *From Goodwill To Grunge*.

Mai, J., n.d. *So Pretty / Very Rotten*. 1st ed. Koyama Press.

Yoshinaga, M. and Ishikawa, K., 2007. *Gothic & Lolita*. London: Phaidon.

Rock, S., n.d. *Young Punks*. 1st ed. Omnibus Press.

Hemingway, W. and Hemingway, G., 2015. *The Vintage Fashion Bible*. David & Charles.

Section 2: Character and Design

Joicey, C. and Nothdruft, D., 2013. *How To Draw Like A Fashion Designer*. London: Thames & Hudson.

Kurtti, J., n.d. *The Art Of Disney Costuming*. 1st ed. Disney Editions.

Pollatsek, S. and Wilson, M., 2017. *Unbuttoned*. New York: Routledge.

Capaccio, N., n.d. *Costume Design In TV And Film*. Cavendish Square Publishing.

La Motte, R., n.d. *Costume Design 101 - The Business And Art Of Creating Costumes For Film And Television*. Michael Wiese Productions.

Clancy Steer, D., n.d. *Designing Costume For Stage And Screen*. Batsford Ltd.

Leese, E., 2013. *Costume Design In The Movies*. New York, NY: Dover Publ.

Section 3: Making Cosplay and What Happens Next

Sewing – Fabric, Patterns and More

Johnston, A. and Hallett, C., 2016. *Fabric For Fashion*. London: Laurence King Publishing.

Smith, A., n.d. *The Sewing Book*. 2nd ed. DK.

2002. *New Complete Guide To Sewing*. London: Reader's Digest.

Lo, D., 2011. *Pattern Cutting*. London: Laurence King.

Richards, A. and Barnfield, J., 2012. *The Pattern Cutting Primer*. London: Bloomsbury.

Kiisel, K., 2016. *Draping*. London: Laurence King Publishing.

Armour Making – Foam, Thermoplastics and Beyond

Quindt, S., 2020. *Kamui Cosplay - Tutorials And Books For Foam And Worbla Cosplay Armor*. [online] KamuiCosplay. Available at: https://www.kamuicosplay.com/

Smith, T., 2020. *The Evil Ted Channel*. [online] The Evil Ted Channel. Available at: https://eviltedsmith.com/

Punished Props Academy. 2020. *Punished Props Academy*. [online] Available at: https://www.punishedprops.com/

Quindt, S., n.d. *The Costume Making Guide*. Impact Books.

Thorsson, S., 2016. *Make Props And Costume Armor*. San Francisco: Maker Media.

Doran, B., n.d. *Foamsmith*

Buying, Commissioning and Modifying

Peacock, R. and Tickner, S., 2015. *Make & Mend*. London: Robinson.

Taylor, J., 2017. *Girl With A Sewing Machine*. Pgw.

Brown, S., 2013. *Refashioned*. London: Laurence King.

Information, M., 2016. *Make Do And Mend*. G2 Rights Ltd.

Mcmurdo, M., n.d. *Upcycling - 20 Creative Projects Made From Reclaimed Materials*. Jacqui Small.

Image Copyrights

Cosplay Images

Megan Amis and Laura King

Historical Images

Rob Hanson
Ted Carnell
Peter Mabey
Elaine Mein
Pam Bucks
Margaret and Bruce Swinyard
Alan Benny